PREFACE

The rapid advancement in Mobile Computing Textbook has revolutionized the way we communicate, work, and live. From smartphones and tablets to wearable devices and smart homes, mobile computing has become an integral part of our daily lives, influencing every domain from healthcare to entertainment. As the field of mobile computing evolves, it becomes essential for students, educators, and professionals to stay updated with both theoretical concepts and practical applications. This textbook, *Mobile Computing: Concepts, Applications, and Exercises*, has been meticulously designed to cater to these needs through a comprehensive and interactive learning approach.

Purpose and Scope

This book aims to provide a holistic understanding of mobile computing by covering fundamental concepts, emerging technologies, and real-world applications. It serves as a one-stop solution for students and professionals pursuing courses in computer science, information technology, and related fields. The content aligns with the syllabi of major universities and institutions, ensuring that learners are well-prepared for academic exams, competitive tests, and professional roles.

Unique Features of the Book

We believe that learning is most effective when it combines theoretical study with practical exercises and multimedia support. To this end, this book offers the following unique features:

1. Comprehensive Theory with Clear Explanations:

Each chapter provides detailed explanations of key concepts, supported by diagrams, flowcharts, and real-world examples to ensure a clear understanding of mobile computing principles.

2. Diverse Exercises:

To reinforce learning and assess comprehension, we have included a variety of exercises:

- **Multiple Choice Questions (MCQs):** Designed to test conceptual clarity and provide practice for competitive exams.
- **True/False:** Helps in quick revision and strengthens factual knowledge.
- **Match the Case:** Improves logical thinking and understanding of relationships between concepts.
- **Jumbled Words and Rearranging Sentences:** Enhances vocabulary and comprehension of technical terms and definitions.

3. Interactive Content and Videos:

Recognizing the importance of visual learning, we have supplemented the book with videos that explain complex topics in an engaging manner. QR codes are provided at the end of relevant chapters, allowing instant access to these resources.

4. Test Papers and Sample Papers:

For practice and self-assessment, a range of test papers, sample papers, and previous years' university papers are included. These are designed to help students familiarize themselves with the exam pattern and improve their time management skills during actual exams.

5. Viva Voce Questions:

To assist students in preparing for viva sessions, we have compiled a list of frequently asked questions. These questions cover both basic and advanced topics, ensuring thorough preparation for oral examinations.

6. University Previous Year Papers:

Understanding the pattern and types of questions asked in exams is crucial for success. We have included previous year papers from multiple universities to give students a clear idea of what to expect and how to approach their exams strategically.

This textbook is ideal for:

- Undergraduate and postgraduate students of computer science, information technology, and related disciplines.
- Educators and trainers looking for a comprehensive resource to aid in teaching mobile computing.
- Professionals who wish to enhance their knowledge of mobile technologies and applications.

Acknowledgments

We extend our sincere gratitude to the subject matter experts, educators, and reviewers who provided invaluable feedback during the development of this textbook. We also thank our team of editors, designers, and multimedia specialists for their tireless efforts in making this book a truly interactive and learner-friendly resource.

We hope this textbook serves as a valuable guide in your journey to mastering mobile computing. Whether you are a student preparing for an exam or a professional seeking to update your knowledge, the exercises, videos, and supplementary materials will provide you with ample opportunities to learn, practice, and excel.

AF792418

Table of Contents

Chapter 1 - Introduction to Mobile Computing

In this chapter you will learn about:

- Definition and Importance of Mobile Computing
- User Mobility and Device Mobility
- Features of Mobile Communication
- Role of Mobile Devices in Modern Computing

Mobile computing has revolutionised how we communicate and access information by enabling mobility and connectivity. This chapter introduces the core concepts of mobile computing, its significance, and the role mobile devices play in modern-day communication networks.

1.1 Definition and Importance of Mobile Computing

Mobile computing refers to using devices wirelessly, allowing users to access data and services anytime, anywhere. It enables real-time communication, data exchange, and seamless mobility across diverse networks and devices, making it an essential component of the digital age.

Importance:

1. **Anywhere, Anytime Connectivity**: Ensures that users stay connected regardless of location.
2. **Enhanced Productivity**: Enables professionals to work and communicate on the go.
3. **Application in Various Fields**: Used in healthcare, education, banking, and entertainment.

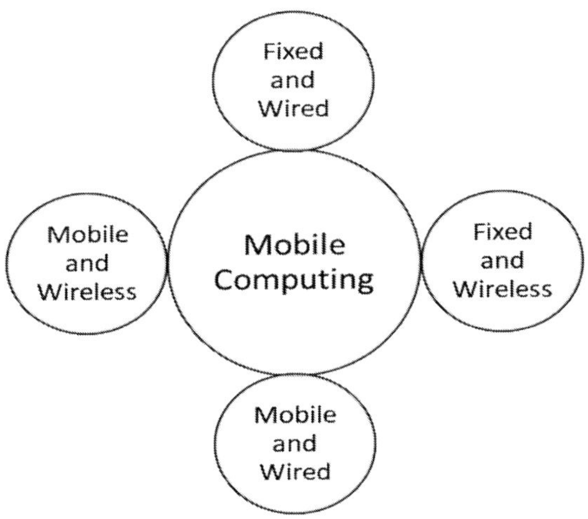

1.2 User Mobility and Device Mobility

a. User Mobility: Refers to the ability of users to move freely while maintaining seamless network connectivity. It focuses on the flexibility to access services without interruption, regardless of the location.

b. Device Mobility: Involves the physical movement of devices across different networks. It ensures the device remains connected while transitioning between various network environments, allowing continuous service availability.

1.3 Features of Mobile Communication

a. Scalability: Mobile systems can expand to support a growing number of users and devices without compromising performance.

b. Network Management: Advanced tools and protocols ensure efficient operation, security, and quality of service in mobile networks.

c. Role-Based Access Control: Security protocols ensure that users and devices have specific access privileges based on their roles.

d. Indoor and Outdoor Coverage: Mobile communication systems offer robust coverage in various settings, ensuring continuous connectivity.

e. Mobile Device Management: Mechanisms like roaming and redundancy ensure that devices can move seamlessly between networks.

1.4 Role of Mobile Devices in Modern Computing

Mobile devices such as smartphones, tablets, and laptops have become integral to personal and professional life. They enable users to:

a. Access information in real-time
b. Perform remote work
c. Engage in mobile banking, e-commerce, and online learning
d. Communicate via voice, text, and video across different platforms
e. Interact with various cloud-based services for data storage and processing

1.5 Glossary

Mobile Computing: Use portable computing devices and wireless networks for real-time communication.
User Mobility: Ability of users to maintain network connectivity while moving.
Device Mobility: The ability of devices to remain connected as they transition between different networks.
Scalability: Capacity of a system to handle increasing loads without performance loss.
Roaming: This process allows a mobile device to remain connected between network regions.
Redundancy: System backup that ensures uninterrupted service during network failures.

1.6 Summary

a. Mobile computing allows access to information and communication services anywhere, anytime.
b. It encompasses both user mobility (focus on the user) and device mobility (focus on the device).
c. Mobile communication offers scalability, efficient network management, and role-based access control to secure data.
d. Mobile devices are critical in modern computing, enabling real-time communication, e-commerce, and cloud services.
e. Advanced mobile communication ensures uninterrupted indoor and outdoor coverage, ensuring high service quality.

1.7 Previous Year Solved Question

Question: Define mobile computing and explain its importance. (IGNOU, December 2022, MCA)

Answer: Mobile Computing refers to the ability to use computing devices wirelessly, enabling users to access data, applications, and services from any location without being restricted to a fixed network or workstation.

Importance:

a. Real-Time Access: Mobile computing allows users to access information and communicate in real-time, which is essential for business operations, social interactions, and emergency services.
b. Seamless Connectivity: Users can remain connected to networks, applications, and services regardless of location.
c. Increased Productivity: Enables employees and individuals to work remotely and efficiently from various locations, improving flexibility and reducing downtime.
d. Enhanced Communication: Mobile devices facilitate instant communication through voice, text, video, and data sharing across multiple platforms.
e. Support for Cloud Services: Mobile computing integrates with cloud-based systems, enabling remote data storage, management, and access.

Exercises

Exercise 1 – Multiple Choice Questions

1. What is Mobile Computing?

a) A type of computing where computers are in a fixed location
b) A type of computing where users can move with their devices
c) A type of computing used only for gaming
d) A technology only for desktop computing

2. Which of the following is a feature of mobile communication?

a) High data transfer speed
b) Fixed location for access
c) High power consumption
d) Wired connection

Exercise 2 – True/False

1. Mobile computing is limited to desktop computers.
2. Device mobility refers to the ability of a device to move between different networks.

Exercise 3 – Fill in the blanks

1. Computing allows users to access data while being ____________.
2. ____________ Mobility refers to the movement of users from one location to another.

Exercise 4 - Fill in the blanks with two options

1. Device mobility allows devices to move between ____________ (networks/regions).
2. Mobile computing has made ____________ (communication/data) more accessible.

Exercise 5 - Rearrange the sentence

1. Communication mobile essential for business is modern.
2. Devices computing portable mobile are an example of

Exercise 6 - Choose the Odd One Out

1. a) Smartphone
   b) Laptop
   c) Landline
   d) Tablet
2. a) GPS
   b) Wi-Fi
   c) Bluetooth
   d) Wired Ethernet

Exercise 7- Jumble words

1. mpuetocr ginviroennm
2. biomytilvedy

Exercise 8- Match case

1. Mobile Computing
2. User Mobility
3. Features of Mobile Communication

a) High data transfer speed
b) Portable devices
c) Movement of users

Exercise 9- Assertion – Reason

1. Assertion: Mobile computing allows users to work while travelling.
Reason: Mobile devices have become lighter and more powerful.
a) Both assertion and reason are true, and the reason is the correct explanation.

b) Both assertion and reason are true, but the reason is not the correct explanation.
c) The assertion is true, but the reason is false.
d) The assertion is false.
2. Assertion: Mobile computing is only used for communication purposes.
Reason: Mobile devices are designed only for calling and texting.
a) Both assertion and reason are true, and the reason is the correct explanation.
b) Both assertion and reason are true, but the reason is not the correct explanation.
c) The assertion is true, but the reason is false.
d) Both assertion and reason are false.

Exercise 10- Read the questions below and find the appropriate word in the provided grid.

M	H	E	L	M	E	T	S	E	T
O	O	Q	W	E	R	T	Y	U	A
B	P	S	D	W	T	Y	G	H	X
I	O	E	R	T	Y	H	S	N	W
L	I	X	C	V	B	N	M	G	V
E	U	F	O	M	N	G	U	N	D
S	Y	I	P	L	U	U	V	J	A
E	H	G	E	K	S	N	X	Z	T
O	G	S	T	J	E	S	W	Y	A
B	O	X	S	V	R	E	S	T	S

Exercise 11- One- word

1. What is the term for the movement of users between different locations?
2. A portable device used for mobile computing.

Exercise 12- Small Answers

1. What is mobile computing?
2. What is user mobility?

Exercise 13- Long Answers

1. Explain the importance of mobile computing in modern business environments.
2. Discuss the role of mobile devices in modern computing.

Exercise 14- Previous Years Unsolved Questions

1. Define mobile computing and explain its key features. (IGNOU, December 2021, MCA)
2. Describe the role of mobile devices in today's computing environment. (Anna University, June 2022, MCA)
3. Define mobile computing and explain its fundamental principles. (Anna University, July 2022, MCA)
4. What are the key components of a mobile computing system? (Anna University, July 2022, MCA)
5. Answer the following questions: (IGNOU, December 2021, MCA)
   a) What is mobile computing?
   b) List two key advantages of mobile computing.
   c) Discuss two challenges associated with mobile computing.
6. Find words/phrases that match the following in the context of mobile computing: (IGNOU, December 2021, MCA)
   a) Mobile application
   b) Data synchronization
   c) Bandwidth limitation
   d) Battery optimization
7. Make sentences using the following mobile computing-related words/phrases: (IGNOU, December 2021, MCA)
   a) Roaming
   b) Mobile broadband
   c) Network latency
   d) Mobile operating system
8. Write short notes on any two of the following: (IGNOU, December 2021, MCA)
   a) Mobile cloud computing

b) Location-based services
c) Mobile device management (MDM)
d) Wearable computing devices

9. Write an email to a friend explaining how you use mobile computing in daily work. (IGNOU, December 2021, MCA)
   a) The apps or software you use
   b) How mobile computing improves your productivity
   c) The role of wireless networks in your work
10. Discuss the ethical considerations in mobile computing, particularly related to data privacy. (Anna University, June 2022, MCA)

Answers

Exercise 1- 1. (b). 2. (a)
Exercise 2- 1. False. 2. True
Exercise 3- 1. Mobile. 2. User
Exercise 4- 1. Networks. 2. Communication
Exercise 5- 1. Mobile communication is essential for modern business.
2. Mobile devices are an example of portable computing.
Exercise 6. 1. (c). 2. (d)
Exercise 7- 1. computing environment. 2. device mobility
Exercise 8- 1. b). 2- c). 3. a)
Exercise 9- 1. (a). 2. (d).
Exercise 10-

M	H	E	L	M	E	T	S	E	T
O	O	Q	W	E	R	T	Y	U	A
B	P	S	D	W	T	Y	G	H	X
I	O	E	R	T	Y	H	S	N	W
L	I	X	C	V	B	N	M	G	V
E	U	F	O	M	N	G	U	N	D
S	Y	I	P	L	**U**	U	V	J	A
E	H	G	E	K	**S**	N	X	Z	T
O	G	S	T	J	**E**	S	W	Y	A
B	O	X	S	V	**R**	E	S	T	S

Exercise 11- 1. User Mobility. 2. Smartphone

Test Paper

Chapter - 1
Introduction to Professional Skills and Ethics

Time Duration: 30 Minutes **Maximum Marks: 25**

General Instructions:

1. The question paper consists of 12 questions and is divided into four sections, A, B, C and D.
2. All questions are compulsory.
3. Section A comprises MCQs, fill in the blanks and True or False carrying one marks each.
4. Section B comprises VSAQs (very short answers questions) carrying two marks each.
5. Section C comprises SAQs (short questions) carrying four marks each.
6. Section D comprises long questions carrying five marks each.

SECTION-A

Q1. Multiple choice questions: **(1*2=2)**

1. What allows mobile devices to remain connected as they transition between networks?
   a) User Mobility
   b) Scalability
   c) Device Mobility
   d) Redundancy
2. What process enables mobile devices to stay connected when moving between different network regions?
   a) Roaming
   b) Redundancy
   c) Scalability
   d) User Mobility

Q2. Fill in the blanks: **(1*2=2)**

1. Mobile computing enables real-time communication and access to information from _____ and _____.
2. _____ ensures uninterrupted service during network failures by having a backup system.

Q3. True or False: **(1*2=2)**

1. Device mobility focuses on ensuring that the user maintains connectivity while moving.
2. Scalability refers to the ability of a system to handle increasing loads without performance loss.

SECTION-B

Q4. Very Short answers type questions-I **(2*3=6)**

1. Define mobile computing.
2. What is the difference between user mobility and device mobility?
3. Why is redundancy important in mobile networks?

SECTION-C

Q5. Short answers type questions-II

1. Explain the role of mobile devices in modern computing and communication.
2. How does scalability contribute to efficient mobile communication management? **(4*2=8)**

SECTION-D

Q6. Long answers type questions **(5*1=5)**

1. Describe how mobile communication enables real-time services and ensures uninterrupted coverage indoors and outdoors.

Chapter 2 - Multiplexing in Mobile Networks

In this chapter you will learn about:

Introduction to Multiplexing
Frequency Division Multiplexing (FDM)
Time Division Multiplexing (TDM)
Wavelength Division Multiplexing (WDM)
Comparison of Multiplexing Techniques

Mobile networks are designed to handle multiple communication signals simultaneously. However, sending multiple signals through the same channel without proper management can lead to interference and degraded performance. Multiplexing is the solution to this challenge. It is a method used to combine multiple signals and send them over a single channel, optimising available bandwidth. This chapter delves into the different types of multiplexing techniques, including Frequency Division Multiplexing (FDM), Time Division Multiplexing (TDM), and Wavelength Division Multiplexing (WDM). Each of these techniques is crucial for improving mobile networks' efficiency, scalability, and performance.
By the end of this chapter, students will understand how multiplexing techniques are applied in mobile communication systems, how they differ, and the benefits and challenges associated with each method.

2.1 Introduction to Multiplexing

Multiplexing is a fundamental technology in telecommunications that allows for the simultaneous transmission of multiple signals over a single communication medium, such as a cable or radio frequency. By combining multiple signals and transmitting them together, multiplexing ensures that the available bandwidth of a communication channel is used efficiently. Each signal is separated at the receiving end through de-multiplexing.
Key points about multiplexing:

a. Maximizes resource utilisation: Rather than dedicating an entire channel to a single signal, multiplexing allows many signals to share the same channel.
b. Minimizes the need for additional infrastructure: Since multiple signals share the same medium, the requirement for additional physical communication channels is reduced.
c. Supports multiple users: Multiplexing techniques are essential in mobile networks where many users communicate simultaneously.
d. Multiplexing is categorized into different types based on how the signals are combined and transmitted, each with its applications and advantages in mobile networks.
e. Frequency Division Multiplexing (FDM)

2.2 Time Division Multiplexing (TDM)

Frequency Division Multiplexing (FDM) is one of the most basic and widely used multiplexing techniques. It works by dividing a communication medium's available bandwidth into smaller frequency bands. Each signal is then transmitted on a unique frequency within these bands.
Key aspects of FDM:
How it works: In FDM, multiple signals are transmitted at different frequencies. Each signal occupies a different portion of the total bandwidth, ensuring they do not interfere.

1. Advantages:
   a. Ideal for continuous signals, such as analog signals in radio or television transmission.
   b. Simple to implement for analog communication.2. Disadvantages:
   a. FDM is susceptible to intermediation interference, where closely spaced frequencies can overlap and cause interference.
   b. It is not bandwidth-efficient when multiple users with varying data transmission rates are present.3. Applications:
   a. Traditional radio broadcasting uses FDM to send radio stations at different frequencies.
   b. Television broadcasting applies FDM to transmit different TV channels over the same transmission medium.In mobile communication, FDM is used in systems where each communication channel is assigned a unique frequency. For example, in early analog cellular systems, FDM played a critical role.

2.3 Wavelength Division Multiplexing (WDM)

Time Division Multiplexing (TDM) operates by dividing the transmission time into intervals or slots. Each signal is allocated a time slot within which it can send data. When the allocated time slot is finished, the system switches to the next signal in the sequence.

Types of TDM:

a. Synchronous TDM: In this type, each signal gets a fixed time slot in each cycle, whether or not the signal has data to send. This method can lead to wasted bandwidth if one or more signals do not use their allocated time slots.

b. Asynchronous TDM: Also called Statistical TDM, this method allocates time slots based on demand. If a signal does not have data to transmit, its slot can be assigned to another signal. This method is more bandwidth-efficient compared to Synchronous TDM.

Advantages:

a. TDM is highly efficient for digital signals, especially when combined with data compression techniques.

b. It ensures that each signal gets a dedicated period for transmission, minimising interference.

Disadvantages:

a. Time synchronization is critical, as delays or mismatches in timing can cause data loss.

b. In high-traffic situations, latency can increase as the system processes multiple signals in sequence.

Applications:

a. TDM is extensively used in digital telephony, where multiple voice signals are multiplexed onto a single communication channel.

b. Cellular networks use TDM in various forms, particularly in second-generation (2G) mobile communication systems.

2.4 Wavelength Division Multiplexing (WDM)

Wavelength Division Multiplexing (WDM) is similar to FDM, but it is used primarily for optical communication systems. In WDM, multiple signals are transmitted at different wavelengths (or colors) of light through an optical fiber. Each wavelength carries a separate data signal.

How it works: WDM involves transmitting several optical signals on the same fiber but at different wavelengths. The system uses different lasers to generate the different wavelengths, which are then combined into a single fiber optic cable.

Advantages:

a. High capacity: WDM offers extremely high data rates and is ideal for long-distance communication.

b. No interference: Since each signal uses a different wavelength of light, there is little risk of interference between signals.

Disadvantages:

a. WDM systems are expensive to deploy due to the complexity of optical components.

b. Requires precise control and monitoring to ensure that wavelengths remain distinct and free from overlap.

Applications:

a. WDM is used in fiber-optic communication for high-capacity data transmission over long distances.

b. It is employed in internet backbone networks and large-scale data centers to handle vast amounts of data traffic.

2.5 Comparison of Multiplexing Techniques

Feature	FDM	TDM	WDM
Primary Use	Analog communication	Digital communication	Optical communication
Channel Separation	Frequency-based	Time-based	Wavelength-based
Advantages	Simple for analog systems	Efficient for digital signals	High capacity, long-distance
Disadvantages	Susceptible to interference	Requires synchronization	Expensive, complex components
Applications	Radio, TV, analog phones	Telephony, 2G, digital phones	Fiber-optic communication

2.6 Glossary

a. Multiplexing: The technique of combining multiple signals to transmit them over a single communication channel.

b. Frequency Division Multiplexing (FDM): Divides bandwidth into separate frequency bands for transmitting multiple signals simultaneously.

c. Time Division Multiplexing (TDM): Divides transmission time into slots, with each signal transmitting in its assigned slot.

d. Wavelength Division Multiplexing (WDM): Optical multiplexing technique that transmits multiple signals on different wavelengths of light through a single fiber.
e. Synchronous TDM: Allocates fixed time slots to each signal, regardless of data presence.
f. Asynchronous TDM: Dynamically allocates time slots based on data transmission demand.

2.7 Summary

a. Multiplexing is essential for the efficient use of communication channels in mobile networks.
b. FDM, TDM, and WDM are the three main types of multiplexing techniques.
c. FDM uses different frequency bands, TDM uses time slots, and WDM uses light wavelengths to transmit multiple signals.
d. Each technique has specific advantages and applications based on the type of communication system (analog, digital, or optical).
e. Understanding the differences between multiplexing techniques is crucial for designing efficient communication systems.

2.8 Previous Year Solved Question

Question: Explain the concept of Frequency Division Multiplexing (FDM), its advantages, disadvantages, and applications in mobile communication. (Anna University, July 2022, MCA)

Answer: Frequency Division Multiplexing (FDM) is a technique for transmitting multiple signals simultaneously over a single communication channel by dividing the available bandwidth into separate frequency bands. Each signal is allocated a unique frequency band within the channel, which is then transmitted simultaneously without interference.

Working of FDM:

a. In FDM, the available bandwidth of the communication medium is divided into smaller frequency bands.
b. Each signal is modulated with a different carrier frequency and transmitted in its frequency band.
c. At the receiving end, a demultiplexer separates the signals based on their frequencies.

Advantages of FDM:

a. Simultaneous transmission: Multiple signals can be transmitted at the same time without interference, which increases the utilization of the available bandwidth.

Continuous transmission: FDM is ideal for analog signals that require continuous transmission, such as audio and video signals in radio and television broadcasting.

1. Simple implementation: FDM is relatively simple to implement for analog communication systems.

Disadvantages of FDM:

1. Intermediation interference: Signals transmitted at closely spaced frequencies may interfere with each other, leading to intermediation interference.
2. Bandwidth inefficiency: FDM is not suitable for digital signals with varying data transmission rates, leading to inefficient bandwidth use.
3. High cost of filtering: FDM requires sophisticated filters to separate closely spaced frequencies, which can be expensive.

Applications of FDM:

- Radio broadcasting: Different radio stations use different frequencies to broadcast their signals.
- Television broadcasting: Multiple television channels are transmitted simultaneously using FDM.
- Analog cellular systems: Early mobile communication systems, such as first-generation (1G) analog cellular systems, used FDM for voice transmission.

Exercises

Exercise 1 – Multiple Choice Questions

1. Which multiplexing technique divides the available bandwidth into separate frequencies?
a. Time Division Multiplexing
b. Frequency Division Multiplexing
c. Wavelength Division Multiplexing
d. Code Division Multiplexing

2. What is the primary purpose of multiplexing in mobile networks?
a. To increase device size
b. To allow multiple signals over a single channel
c. To separate data packets
d. To reduce network speed

Exercise 2 – True/False

1. Frequency Division Multiplexing (FDM) assigns different time slots for each channel.
2. In Time Division Multiplexing (TDM), each user is allocated a unique frequency.

Exercise 3 – Fill in the blanks

1. ____________ Multiplexing assigns each user a unique frequency range.
2. Time Division Multiplexing allows multiple signals by dividing time into ____________.

Exercise 4- Fill in the blanks with two options

1. Wavelength Division Multiplexing (WDM) is mainly used in ____________ (optical/frequency)
2. Communication in FDM, different signals are sent over different ____________ (frequencies/times).

Exercise 5- Rearrange the sentence

1. Communication allows signals multiplexing efficient through.
2. Transmitted each with signal it is in multiplexing division frequency.

Exercise 6- Choose the Odd One Out

a. Frequency Division Multiplexing
b. Time Division Multiplexing
c. Code Division Multiplexing
d. Database Management

a. FDM
b. Optical Fiber
c. 0TDM
d. WDM

Exercise 7- Jumble words

1. pidvion ivosinid ftqrueenyc
2. meit onsvidi tipmuxelg

Exercise 8- Match case

1. Frequency Division Multiplexing (FDM)
2. Time Division Multiplexing (TDM)
3. Wavelength Division Multiplexing (WDM)

a) Uses different light wavelengths
b) Divides time into slots
c) Divides bandwidth into frequencies

Exercise 9- Assertion – Reason

1. Assertion: FDM allows multiple users to share the same frequency channel.
Reason: FDM assigns unique frequency ranges to each user.
a. Both assertion and reason are true, and the reason is the correct explanation.
b. Both assertion and reason are true, but the reason is not the correct explanation.
c. The assertion is true, but the reason is false.
d. Both assertion and reason are false.

2. Assertion: WDM is primarily used in fibre-optic communications.
Reason: WDM relies on dividing signals by time slots.
a. Both assertion and reason are true, and the reason is the correct explanation.
b. Both assertion and reason are true, but the reason is not the correct explanation.
c. The assertion is true, but the reason is false.
d. Both assertion and reason are false.

Exercise 10- Read the questions below and find the appropriate word in the provided grid.

M	H	F	L	M	E	T	S	F	T
U	O	R	W	E	R	T	Y	U	A
L	P	E	D	W	T	Y	G	D	X
T	O	Q	R	T	Y	H	S	I	W
I	I	U	C	V	B	N	M	V	V
P	U	E	O	M	N	G	U	I	D
L	Y	N	P	L	U	U	V	S	A
E	H	C	E	K	S	N	X	I	T
X	G	Y	T	J	E	S	W	O	A
S	O	X	S	V	R	E	S	N	S

Exercise 11- One- word

1. What is the process of dividing communication channels for multiple users called?
2. Which multiplexing method divides a single channel into separate time slots?

Exercise 12- Small Answers

1. What is Frequency Division Multiplexing (FDM)?
2. Explain the purpose of Time Division Multiplexing (TDM).

Exercise 13- Long Answers

1. Compare Frequency Division Multiplexing (FDM) and Time Division Multiplexing (TDM).
2. Describe Wavelength Division Multiplexing (WDM) and its applications.

Exercise 14- Previous Years Unsolved Questions

1. Define and explain the significance of multiplexing in mobile networks. (Anna University, July 2022, MCA)
2. How do WDM and TDM differ, and in which scenarios would each be used? (Mumbai University, December 2023, MCA)
3. Explain the challenges of mobile application testing and quality assurance. (Mumbai University, December 2023, MCA)
4. What is the role of mobile computing in social networking? (IGNOU, December 2021, MCA)
5. Describe the process of app store optimization for mobile applications. (Anna University, June 2022, MCA.
6. How does mobile computing support real-time data processing? (Anna University, July 2022, MCA)
7. Discuss the ethical issues surrounding mobile app data collection. (IGNOU, December 2021, MCA)
8. What is the role of artificial intelligence in enhancing mobile computing applications? (Mumbai University, December 2023, MCA)
9. Explain the role of 5G in enabling advanced mobile computing solutions. (Anna University, June 2022, MCA)

Answers

Exercise 1- 1. (b). 2. (b)
Exercise 2- 1. False. 2. False
Exercise 3- 1. Frequency Division. 2. slot
Exercise 4- 1. Optical. 2. Frequencies
Exercise 5- 1. Multiplexing allows efficient communication through signals.
2. In Frequency Division Multiplexing, each signal is transmitted with its own frequency.
Exercise 6- 1. (d). 2. (b)
Exercise 7- 1. Frequency Division Multiplexing. 2. Time Division Multiplexing
Exercise 8- 1. C. 2. B 3. A
Exercise 9- 1. C. 2. C
Exercise 10-

M	H	**F**	L	M	E	T	S	F	T
U	O	**R**	W	E	R	T	Y	U	A
L	P	**E**	D	W	T	Y	G	**D**	X
T	O	**Q**	R	T	Y	H	S	**I**	W
I	I	**U**	C	V	B	N	M	**V**	V
P	U	**E**	O	M	N	G	U	**I**	D
L	Y	**N**	P	L	U	U	V	**S**	A
E	H	**C**	E	K	S	N	X	**I**	T
X	G	**Y**	T	J	E	S	W	**O**	A
S	O	X	S	V	R	E	S	**N**	S

Exercise 11- 1. Multiplexing 2. TDM

Test Paper
Chapter-2
Multiplexing in Mobile Networks

Time Duration: 30 Minutes **Maximum Marks: 25**

General Instructions:

1. The question paper consists of 12 questions and is divided into four sections, A, B, C and D.
2. All questions are compulsory.
3. Section A comprises MCQs, fill in the blanks and True or False carrying one marks each.
4. Section B comprises VSAQs (very short answers questions) carrying two marks each.
5. Section C comprises SAQs (short questions) carrying four marks each.
6. Section D comprises long questions carrying five marks each.

SECTION-A

Q1. Multiple choice questions: **(1*2=2)**

1. Which multiplexing technique divides bandwidth into frequency bands?

a) TDM
b) FDM
c) WDM
d) Asynchronous TDM

2. What type of multiplexing uses different wavelengths of light to transmit signals?

a) TDM
b) WDM
c) FDM
d) Synchronous TDM

Q2. Fill in the blanks: **(1*2=2)**

1. _____ multiplexing dynamically allocates time slots based on data transmission demand.
2. _____ is an optical multiplexing technique that uses light wavelengths for transmission.

Q3. True or False: **(1*2=2)**

1. Synchronous TDM allocates time slots only when data is available for transmission.
2. Multiplexing allows multiple signals to share a single communication channel.

SECTION-B

Q4. Very Short answers type questions-I **(2*3=6)**

1. Define multiplexing.
2. What is the main difference between synchronous and asynchronous TDM?
3. Name one application of wavelength division multiplexing (WDM).

SECTION-C

Q5. Short answers type questions-II **(4*2=8)**

1. Explain the differences between FDM, TDM, and WDM.
2. Why is multiplexing important in mobile networks?

SECTION-D

Q6. Long answers type questions **(5*1=5)**

1. Describe the role of multiplexing techniques in communication systems, and explain the advantages of using these techniques.

Chapter 3 - Evolution of Mobile Communication Systems

In this chapter you will learn about:
- History and Evolution of Mobile
- Networks
- Global System for Mobile
- Communication
- Overview of 1G and 2G Networks
- GPRS and 2.5G Technology

The evolution of mobile communication systems reflects the transformation of wireless technology over the decades, moving from basic analogy voice services to complex digital networks that support high-speed data and multimedia communication. This chapter delves into the history, development, and major technological advances in mobile networks.

3.1 History and Evolution of Mobile Networks

The evolution of mobile networks can be categorized into several stages, starting from simple analogy communication systems to advanced digital networks. The initial mobile communication systems were mainly limited to voice transmission. Over time, technological advancements introduced digital systems, allowing for higher-quality voice communication and, eventually, data transmission capabilities.

a. 0G (Pre-Cellular): Before cellular networks, mobile communication was limited to large, radio-based mobile phones used in public transportation and emergency services. These systems were costly, with limited range and mobility.

b. 1G (First Generation): The introduction of the first cellular networks in the 1980s marked a transition to analogy technology. 1G enabled voice communication between mobile phones and the public switched telephone network (PSTN), offering improved range and coverage. However, these networks lacked security and were prone to interference.

c. 2G (Second Generation): The transition to digital technology began in the early 1990s with the second generation (2G) of mobile networks. Digital technology improved voice quality and introduced additional features such as Short Messaging Service (SMS) and higher security. The introduction of the Global System for Mobile Communication (GSM) standardised mobile communication across countries and improved network capacity.

3.2 Overview of 1G and 2G Networks

I. 1G Networks

a. Technology: 1G network relied on analogy transmission, allowing essential voice services through frequency division multiple accesses (FDMA).

b. Limitations: Poor voice quality, lack of encryption, and vulnerability to interference. 1G devices were large, had limited battery life, and lacked handoff capabilities, limiting user mobility across different cell towers.

c. Use Cases: Mainly voice calls, with limited scalability.

II. 2G Networks

a. Introduction of Digital Transmission: 2G networks represented a shift from analogy to digital communication. These systems employed digital encryption, improving call security and voice quality.

b. GSM Standard: The GSM (Global System for Mobile Communications) standard was widely adopted, increasing compatibility and allowing for international roaming.

c. New Services: Besides improved voice quality, 2G enabled SMS messaging, allowing short text messages to be sent between mobile devices. These networks used time division multiple access (TDMA) and code division multiple access (CDMA) technologies to increase network efficiency and capacity.

3.3 Global System for Mobile Communication (GSM)

Introduction: GSM is a globally recognised standard for digital cellular networks, introduced in the early 1990s. It revolutionised mobile communication by allowing users to switch networks and roam internationally.

GSM Architecture: GSM is based on a well-structured architecture that includes several essential components:

1. **Mobile Station (MS):** The mobile device or handset the user uses.
2. **Base Station Subsystem (BSS):** Manages communication between the mobile device and the network.
3. **Network and Switching Subsystem (NSS):** Responsible for call management and mobility.
4. **Operations Support System (OSS):** Maintains and manages the network infrastructure.

Key Features of GSM:

1. **Digital Encryption:** Provides better security for voice and data.
2. **International Roaming:** Standardized protocols enable seamless communication across different GSM networks worldwide.

3. **Scalability:** GSM networks can handle many users, making them ideal for densely populated areas.

3.4 GPRS and 2.5G Technology

General Packet Radio Service (GPRS): An enhancement to 2G, GPRS enabled mobile internet access, marking a step towards high-speed data transmission. This technology, known as 2.5G, allowed mobile phones to access online services such as web browsing, email, and multimedia messaging.

Key Features of GPRS:

1. **Packet-Switched Technology:** GPRS used packet-switching to transmit data efficiently over existing GSM networks.
2. **Enhanced Data Rates:** GPRS achieved up to 114 Kbps speeds, significantly faster than 2G's circuit-switched connections.
3. **Always-On Connection:** Users could stay connected without needing to dial in repeatedly.

Impact of 2.5G: By bridging the gap between 2G and 3G, GPRS allowed mobile internet services, giving users early access to features like multimedia messaging and real-time access to information on the go.

3.5 Glossary

1. **1G:** The first generation of analogy mobile networks primarily focused on voice communication.
2. **2G:** Second-generation digital mobile networks, enabling SMS and improved call quality.
3. **GSM:** A global standard for digital cellular networks, offering interoperability and security.
4. **GPRS:** General Packet Radio Service, a packet-switched enhancement to 2G enabling mobile internet.
5. **Roaming:** The ability for a mobile device to access network services outside its home network.

3.6 Summary

- The evolution from analogy to digital mobile networks has drastically improved call quality, security, and capacity.
- GSM played a crucial role in standardising mobile communication, making mobile telephony more accessible globally.
- The introduction of GPRS marked the beginning of mobile internet access, allowing users to access online services over mobile networks.
- Each generation of mobile networks introduced advancements that improved communication quality, data services, and security.

3.7 Previous Years Solved Question

Question: Explain the evolution of mobile networks from 1G to 2.5G and their main characteristics. (Anna University, June 2022, MCA)

Answer: The development of mobile networks from 1G to 2.5G represents a significant transformation in communication technology, shifting from basic analogy systems to more sophisticated digital networks that paved the way for mobile internet. Here is an in-depth look at the evolution of these generations and their defining characteristics:

1G (First Generation) - Analog Voice Communication

1G represents the first generation of mobile networks, introduced in the early 1980s, and was entirely based on analogy technology. These networks were designed to provide basic voice communication services without data transmission capabilities.

The key features of 1G included:

- **Analog Signal Transmission**: 1G network used analogy technology, which had limitations regarding call quality, interference, and security.
- **FDMA Technology**: Frequency Division Multiple Access (FDMA) was used to allocate individual channels to users, but this method limited the number of users in each cell and was less efficient than later technologies.
- **Low Security and High Interference**: Calls on 1G network were vulnerable to eavesdropping and interference, as analogy signals could be easily intercepted.
- **Poor Voice Quality and Limited Coverage:** 1G systems struggled with poor voice quality and limited coverage, and the analogy signals degraded over longer distances.
- **Limited Mobility**: The handoff between cells was manual, restricting user mobility and making it difficult for users to move freely while staying connected.

Overall, 1G networks offered a rudimentary foundation for mobile telephony but fell short in quality, security, and scalability.

2G (Second Generation) - Digital Transformation

Introduced in the early 1990s, 2G marked the transition from analogy to digital communication and significantly improved mobile networks. This generation addressed the shortcomings of 1G and enabled additional services. The characteristics of 2G include:

- **Digital Transmission:** Unlike 1G, 2G used digital signals, which improved voice quality, reduced interference, and introduced encryption for enhanced security.
- **GSM Standardization**: The Global System for Mobile Communications (GSM) became the global standard for 2G networks, allowing for interoperability between networks in different countries and the beginning of international roaming.
- **TDMA and CDMA Technologies:** 2G networks utilised Time Division Multiple Access (TDMA) and Code Division Multiple Access (CDMA), which allowed multiple users to share the same frequency band, increasing network capacity.
- **New Services – SMS and MMS:** 2G enabled text messaging (SMS), which became an instant hit, and Multimedia Messaging Service (MMS) allowed users to share images and audio files, expanding communication beyond voice.
- **Improved Call Security:** Digital encryption techniques made communication more secure and reliable, enhancing user privacy.
- **Extended Battery Life:** 2G devices were more power-efficient than 1G devices, thanks to the digital signals, which consumed less power.

The introduction of 2G brought enhanced security, interoperability, and new messaging capabilities, making mobile phones widely accessible and usable daily.

2.5G - Transition to Data Services with GPRS

The advent of 2.5G was a significant step forward, as it introduced packet-switched data transmission on top of the existing 2G infrastructure, which was primarily circuit-switched. This transition enabled mobile internet use, setting the stage for modern data services.

The characteristics of 2.5G networks include:

- **GPRS Technology:** General Packet Radio Service (GPRS) was introduced to enhance 2G networks, allowing data to be transmitted in packets. This enabled a faster and more efficient way to handle data transmission than circuit-switched methods.
- **Mobile Internet Access:** GPRS allows users to access the internet, browse web pages, check emails, and even download small files. This began mobile data usage, which later generations would build upon.
- **Always-On Connectivity:** Unlike the dial-up model of circuit-switched connections, GPRS allowed for an "always-on" connection, meaning users could stay connected to the network without repeatedly dialling in.
- **Higher Data Speeds:** GPRS could achieve data speeds between 56 Kbps and 114 Kbps, significantly faster than 2G's 9.6 Kbps and allowing basic internet access.
- **Expanded Services:** GPRS also supported multimedia messaging, allowing users to send and receive pictures, audio files, and other forms of media, which was groundbreaking at the time.

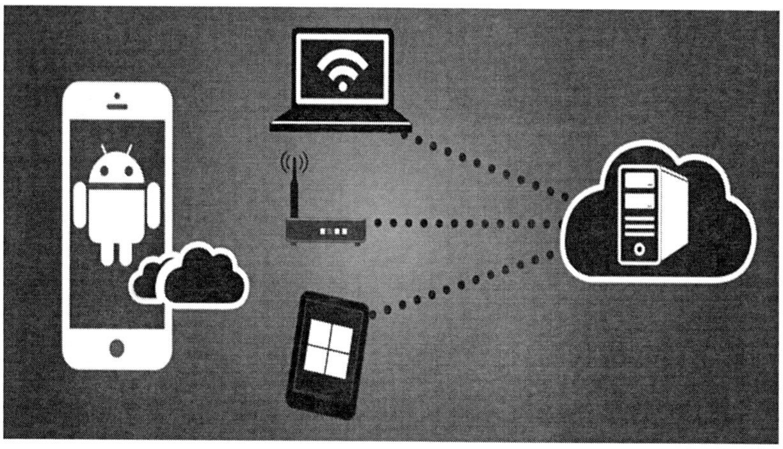

Exercises

Exercise 1 – Multiple Choice Questions

1. What does GPRS stand for?

a) General Protocol Radio Service
b) General Packet Radio Service
c) Global Packet Radio Standard
d) General Phone Radio Service

2. Which network standard marked the beginning of mobile internet access?

a) GSM
b) 1G
c) GPRS
d) 2G

Exercise 2 – True/False

1. GSM enabled global interoperability for mobile networks.
2. 2G was the first network generation to offer internet access to mobile users.

Exercise 3 – Fill in the blanks

1. _____ marked the beginning of mobile internet access over mobile networks.
2. _____ is the first generation of analog mobile networks.

Exercise 4 - Fill in the blanks with two options

1. The _____ (GSM/1G) standard provided better call quality and security compared to earlier analog networks.
2. GPRS is an enhancement to _____ (1G/2G) networks for mobile internet access.

Exercise 5- Rearrange the sentence

1. Call / networks / mobile / quality / improved / the evolution of digital / drastically.
2. A / for / standard / important / GSM / was / mobile communication.

Exercise 6- Choose the Odd One Out

1. a) GSM
b) GPRS
c) Roaming
d) SMS
2. a) 1G
b) 2G
c) GPRS
d) Analog

Exercise 7- Jumble words

1. GPERS (Hint: Mobile internet access)
2. SSGM (Hint: Standard for mobile networks)

Exercise 8- Match case

1. 1G
2. GPRS
3. GSM
4. Roaming

a) Introduction of mobile internet access
b) First generation of analog networks
c) Global standard for mobile networks
d) Ability to access networks outside home

Exercise 9- Assertion – Reason

1. **Assertion:** GSM allowed mobile communication to become globally accessible.
Reason: GSM was the first analog mobile network.
a) Both assertion and reason are true, and the reason is the correct explanation of the assertion.
b) Both assertion and reason are true, but the reason is not the correct explanation of the assertion.
c) Assertion is true, but the reason is false.
d) Both assertion and reason are false.
2. **Assertion:** 2G networks improved call quality and security.
Reason: 2G networks are packet-switched.
a) Both assertion and reason are true, and the reason is the correct explanation of the assertion.
b) Both assertion and reason are true, but the reason is not the correct explanation of the assertion.
c) Assertion is true, but the reason is false.
d) Both assertion and reason are false.

Exercise 10- Read the questions below and find the appropriate word in the provided grid.

1. What is a feature that allows a mobile phone user to make and receive calls, send and receive messages, and access data while outside of their wireless provider's coverage area?
2. What to define protocols for 2 G networks. It operated as a substitute for the 1 G cellular network?

M	H	F	L	M	E	T	S	F	T
U	O	R	W	E	R	T	Y	U	A
L	P	E	D	W	T	Y	G	D	X
T	O	Q	R	T	Y	H	S	I	W
I	I	U	C	V	B	N	M	V	V
P	U	E	O	M	N	G	U	I	D
L	Y	N	P	L	U	U	V	S	A
E	H	C	E	K	S	N	X	I	T
X	G	Y	T	J	E	S	W	O	A
S	O	X	S	V	R	E	S	N	S

Exercise 11- One- word

1. What network enhancement allowed mobile internet access over 2G networks?
2. Which global standard improved security and interoperability in mobile networks?

Exercise 12- Small Answers

1. Explain the role of GSM in the evolution of mobile networks.
2. What were the key improvements introduced with 2G networks?

Exercise 13- Long Answers

1. Describe the evolution from analog to digital mobile networks and the improvements it brought.
2. How did GPRS revolutionize mobile communication, and what impact did it have on mobile internet access?

Exercise 14- Previous Years Unsolved Questions

1. Discuss the importance of battery life in mobile computing. What are some methods to improve battery performance? (IGNOU, December 2021, MCA)
2. What is the impact of mobile computing on businesses? Provide real-world examples. (Anna University, June 2022, MCA)
3. Describe the architecture of a mobile computing environment. (Mumbai University, December 2023, MCA)
4. How does mobile apps access cloud services in a mobile computing environment? Explain with an example. (IGNOU, December 2021, MCA)
5. What is mobile data offloading, and why is it important in mobile computing? (Anna University, June 2022, MCA)
6. Explain the security challenges faced by mobile computing devices and how they can be mitigated. (Anna University, July 2022, MCA)
7. What is context-aware computing, and how is it applied in mobile computing? (Mumbai University, December 2023, MCA)

Answers

Exercise 1- 1. b) General Packet Radio Service. 2. c) GPRS
Exercise 2- 1. True. 2. False
Exercise 3- 1. GPRS. 2. 1G
Exercise 4- 1. GSM. 2. 2G
Exercise 5- 1. The evolution of digital mobile networks drastically improved call quality.
2. GSM was an important standard for mobile communication.
Exercise 6. 1. d) SMS. 2. d) Analog
Exercise 7- 1. GPRS. 2. GSM
Exercise 8- 1 – b. 2 – a. 3 – c. 4 - d
Exercise 9- 1. c) Assertion is true, but the reason is false. 2. c) Assertion is true, but the reason is false.
Exercise 10-

M	H	F	L	M	E	T	S	F	T
U	O	**R**	**O**	**A**	**M**	**I**	**N**	**G**	A
L	P	E	D	W	T	Y	**G**	D	X
T	O	Q	R	T	Y	H	**S**	I	W
I	I	U	C	V	B	N	**M**	V	V
P	U	E	O	M	N	G	U	I	D
L	Y	N	P	L	U	U	V	S	A
E	H	C	G	S	M	N	X	I	T
X	G	Y	T	J	E	S	W	O	A
S	O	X	S	V	R	E	S	N	S

Exercise 11- 1. GPRS. 2. GSM

Test Paper

Chapter-3
Evolution of Mobile Communication Systems

Time Duration: 30 Minutes **Maximum Marks: 25**

General Instructions:
1. The question paper consists of 12 questions and is divided into four sections, A, B, C and D.
2. All questions are compulsory.
3. Section A comprises MCQs, fill in the blanks and True or False carrying one marks each.
4. Section B comprises VSAQs (very short answers questions) carrying two marks each.
5. Section C comprises SAQs (short questions) carrying four marks each.
6. Section D comprises long questions carrying five marks each.

SECTION-A

Q1. Multiple choice questions: **(1*2=2)**

1. What mobile network standard introduced mobile internet access?

a) 2G
b) 1G
c) GPRS
d) GSM

2. Which generation of mobile networks focused primarily on analog voice communication?

a) 2G
b) 1G
c) GSM
d) 3G

Q2. Fill in the blanks: **(1*2=2)**
1. _____ is a global standard for digital cellular networks, ensuring interoperability and security.
2. _____ allows a mobile device to remain connected while accessing network services outside its home network.

Q3. True or False: **(1*2=2)**
1. The introduction of 2G enabled SMS and improved call quality.
2. GPRS is an enhancement to GSM enabling high-speed video streaming.

SECTION-B

Q4. Very Short answers type questions-I **(2*3=6)**
1. What role did GSM play in mobile communication?
2. How did GPRS improve mobile networks?
3. What is the primary focus of 1G mobile network?

SECTION-C

Q5. Short answers type questions-II **(4*2=8)**
1. Compare the key features of 1G and 2G mobile networks.
2. How has the evolution of mobile networks improved communication quality and security?

SECTION-D

Q6. Long answers type questions **(5*1=5)**
1. Explain the impact of different mobile network generations (1G to GPRS) on communication and data services.

Chapter 4 - Third and Fourth Generation (3G & 4G) Networks

In this chapter you will learn about:

- Introduction to 3G Networks
- Features and Applications of 3G
- Introduction to 4G Networks
- Long-Term Evolution (LTE) Technology
- Advantages and Disadvantages of 3G & 4G

The progression from third-generation (3G) to fourth-generation (4G) networks marked a significant leap forward in mobile technology, with enhanced data speeds, improved connectivity, and expanded multimedia capabilities. These advancements were instrumental in fostering the growth of mobile applications, video streaming, and high-speed internet access on mobile devices.

4.1 Introduction to 3G Networks

3G, or the Third Generation of mobile networks, represented a major evolution over 2G, focusing on providing high-speed data transmission and supporting multimedia services. Introduced in the early 2000s, 3G networks brought substantial improvements in internet connectivity and the ability to transfer large amounts of data.

1. **Data Speed:** 3G supported data speeds ranging from 200 Kbps to several Mbps, enabling faster web browsing, video calling, and basic video streaming.
2. **UMTS Standard:** Universal Mobile Telecommunications System (UMTS) became the key 3G standard, alongside CDMA2000 and EDGE in some regions.
3. **Multimedia and Applications:** 3G made applications like video conferencing, multimedia messaging (MMS), and mobile gaming more accessible, fostering the growth of mobile apps and services.

4.2 Features and Applications of 3G

3G introduced various features that laid the foundation for future mobile services. Some of the most notable features and applications include:

- **High-Speed Data Transmission**: 3G networks offered faster data speeds than 2G, supporting mobile email, browsing, and early video streaming applications.
- Video Calling: Mobile users can now engage in real-time video calls, paving the way for personal and professional communication enhancements.
- **Mobile Television and Streaming**: 3G made mobile streaming possible, allowing users to access live TV and stream media on their devices.
- **Increased Security:** Enhanced encryption and authentication methods improved data security on mobile devices.

4.3 Introduction to 4G Networks

The Fourth Generation (4G) networks, launched around 2010, focused on meeting the growing demand for data and multimedia services. 4G networks were designed with an all-IP-based infrastructure, allowing faster data transfer rates and seamless connectivity.

- **Speed:** 4G networks offered data speeds of 100 Mbps to 1 Gbps, enabling smooth HD video streaming, mobile gaming, and high-definition video calling.
- **OFDM Technology:** Orthogonal Frequency-Division Multiplexing (OFDM) divides data streams into smaller signals for better handling and speed.
- **All-IP Network:** 4G introduced an all-IP architecture, ensuring efficient transmission of voice, video, and data through the Internet protocol. This enabled VoIP services like Skype and, later, mobile voice-over-LTE (VoLTE).
- **Seamless Global Connectivity:** 4G allows users to access their data seamlessly across devices and networks, enhancing the overall mobile experience.

4.4 Long-Term Evolution (LTE) Technology

LTE (Long-Term Evolution) is an advanced standard in 4G technology designed to deliver high-speed wireless communication. Often referred to as 4G LTE, this technology improves the speed, quality, and capacity of mobile networks, allowing users to experience seamless internet connectivity.

- Higher Data Rates: LTE provided peak download speeds up to 300 Mbps and upload speeds up to 75 Mbps.
- Reduced Latency: Lower latency improved the performance of applications such as gaming, video calling, and real-time data transfer.

- VoLTE: Voice over LTE (VoLTE) enabled high-definition voice quality over IP networks, improving call clarity compared to previous generations.
- Better Capacity Handling: LTE's high capacity supported more users per cell tower, addressing the surge in mobile device usage and data consumption.

4.5 Advantages and Disadvantages of 3G & 4G

Advantages of 3G:

- **Faster Speeds:** Supported faster internet and data transfer speeds than 2G.
- **Enhanced Multimedia Services:** Enabled video calls, multimedia messaging, and mobile gaming.
- **Wider Coverage**: 3G expanded mobile coverage, especially in urban areas, improving connectivity.

Disadvantages of 3G:

- **Limited Speed:** While faster than 2G, 3G speeds were still insufficient for heavy data applications like HD streaming.
- **Higher Costs:** Higher data usage costs and limited network availability in rural areas limited 3G's reach.

Advantages of 4G:

- **High Data Rates:** Supports high-speed browsing, HD streaming, and seamless video calls.
- **Reduced Latency:** Real-time applications like online gaming and video conferencing are ideal.
- **Wider Coverage**: 4G networks expanded coverage, reaching more users worldwide.

Disadvantages of 4G:

- **Battery Consumption**: High-speed networks consume more battery power on mobile devices.
- **Infrastructure Costs:** Upgrading to 4G required significant investments from telecom providers, affecting availability in some regions.

4.6 Glossary

- **3G**: Third Generation of mobile networks, focused on improving data speeds and introducing multimedia capabilities.
- **4G:** Fourth Generation of mobile networks, offering higher data speeds and supporting HD streaming, online gaming, and more.
- **LTE:** Long-Term Evolution, a high-speed wireless standard in 4G networks.
- **VoLTE:** Voice over LTE is a technology that allows voice calls to be made over LTE networks with improved audio quality.
- **OFDM:** Orthogonal Frequency-Division Multiplexing used in 4G networks to transmit data more efficiently.

4.7 Summary

- **3G Networks:** Introduced high-speed data, multimedia messaging, and video calling, enabling various mobile applications.
- **4G Networks:** Brought ultra-fast data speeds, IP-based infrastructure, and services like HD streaming and VoLTE.
- **LTE Technology:** Enhanced 4G networks with faster speeds, reduced latency, and better handling of high-capacity data demands.
- **Advantages of 3G & 4G**: Included high data speeds, improved voice quality, and more extensive coverage, although 4G was a major leap in connectivity.
- **Disadvantages:** Both networks required significant infrastructure upgrades, with 4G especially power-intensive for devices.

4.8 Previous Year Solved Question

Question: Explain the evolution from 3G to 4G technology. What are the major improvements and new features introduced with 4G? (Mumbai University, December 2023, MCA)

Answer: The evolution from 3G to 4G marked a significant leap in mobile technology, focused on data speeds, efficiency, and multimedia capabilities. Key advancements include:

- Higher Data Speeds: 3G networks provided speeds up to a few Mbps, whereas 4G offered speeds up to 1 Gbps, enabling seamless HD video streaming, faster browsing, and improved mobile gaming.
- All-IP Network: 4G introduced an all-IP-based infrastructure that improved efficiency, voice-over-IP services, and supported applications like VoLTE.
- Low Latency: 4G networks significantly reduced latency, enhancing real-time applications like video conferencing and online gaming.
- Capacity and Scalability: 4G's advanced infrastructure allowed more users per cell tower, managing the increasing demand for mobile data.

Exercises

Exercise 1 – Multiple Choice Questions

1. What does VoLTE stand for?

a) Voice over Long-Term Evolution
b) Video over LTE
c) Voice Optimization LTE
d) Virtual Operation LTE

2. Which technology is used in 4G networks for efficient data transmission?

a) LTE
b) OFDM
c) VoLTE
d) 3G

Exercise 2 – True/False

1. LTE is part of the 3G mobile network.
2. 4G networks support HD streaming and online gaming.

Exercise 3 – Fill in the blanks

1. _____ Networks brought ultra-fast data speeds and VoLTE services.
2. _____ is a technology used in 4G networks to enhance data transmission efficiency.

Exercise 4- Fill in the blanks with two options

1. VoLTE improves audio quality by transmitting voice over _____ (3G/LTE) networks.
2. The _____ (3G/4G) network introduced video calling and multimedia messaging.

Exercise 5- Rearrange the sentence

1. LTE / of / standard / A / 4G / high-speed / is.
2. Improved / 4G / quality / speeds / HD / and / audio / data / services.

Exercise 6- Choose the Odd One Out

1. a) LTE
b) VoLTE
c) OFDM
d) 3G
2. a) HD Streaming
b) Online Gaming
c) Multimedia Messaging
d) SMS

Exercise 7- Jumble words

1. ODFM (Hint: Used in 4G networks)
2. TLE (Hint: High-speed wireless standard in 4G)

Exercise 8- Match case

1. 3G
2. LTE
3. VoLTE
4. 4G

a) High-speed wireless standard in 4G
b) Technology for making voice calls over LTE
c) Introduced video calling and multimedia
d) Supports HD streaming and online gaming

Exercise 9- Assertion – Reason

1. **Assertion:** VoLTE improves voice call quality over LTE networks.
Reason: VoLTE is part of the 3G infrastructure.
a) Both assertion and reason are true, and the reason is the correct explanation.
b) Both assertion and reason are true, but the reason is not the correct explanation.
c) Assertion is true, but the reason is false.
d) Both assertion and reason are false.

2. **Assertion:** 4G networks are power-intensive for devices.
Reason: 4G networks support IP-based services and HD streaming.
a) Both assertion and reason are true, and the reason is the correct explanation.
b) Both assertion and reason are true, but the reason is not the correct explanation.
c) Assertion is true, but the reason is false.
d) Both assertion and reason are false.

Exercise 10- Read the questions below and find the appropriate word in the provided grid.

1. Find the high-speed wireless standard used in 4G networks.
2. Identify the technology that enables voice calls over LTE networks.

M	H	F	L	M	E	T	S	F	T
U	O	R	W	E	R	T	Y	U	A
L	P	E	D	W	T	Y	G	D	X
T	O	Q	R	T	Y	H	S	I	W
I	I	U	C	V	B	N	M	V	V
P	U	E	O	M	N	G	U	I	D
L	Y	N	P	L	U	U	V	S	A
E	H	C	E	K	S	N	X	I	T
X	G	Y	T	J	E	S	W	O	A
S	O	X	S	V	R	E	S	N	S

Exercise 11- One- word

1. What does LTE stand for?
2. Which technology enables voice calls over LTE networks?

Exercise 12- Small Answers

1. Explain how 4G networks are an improvement over 3G.
2. What role does VoLTE play in modern communication?

Exercise 13- Long Answers

1. Describe the differences between 3G and 4G networks in terms of speed, services, and infrastructure.
2. What are the advantages and disadvantages of 3G and 4G networks?

Exercise 14- Previous Years Unsolved Questions

1. What are mobile computing frameworks? Provide examples and their applications. (Anna University, June 2022, MCA)
2. Define mobile device management (MDM). Why is it crucial for enterprises using mobile computing? (Anna University, July 2022, MCA)
3. Explain the term "location-based services" in mobile computing. What are its applications? (IGNOU, December 2021, MCA)
4. How has mobile computing transformed healthcare? Provide examples of mobile health applications. (Mumbai University, December 2023, MCA)
5. Discuss the importance of bandwidth management in mobile computing networks. (Anna University, June 2022, MCA)
6. What are the main differences between 4G and 5G in mobile computing? (Anna University, July 2022, MCA)
7. Describe the role of sensors in mobile devices and how they enhance user experience. (IGNOU, December 2021, MCA)
8. Write short notes on: (IGNOU, December 2021, MCA)
i. Mobile augmented reality
ii. Mobile virtual reality

iii. Mobile payment systems

9. Explain how Bluetooth technology is used in mobile computing. Provide examples of its applications. (Anna University, June 2022, MCA)

10. How do mobile devices handle data synchronization in a mobile computing environment? (Anna University, July 2022, MCA)

11. Describe the mobile computing lifecycle, from app development to deployment. (IGNOU, December 2021, MCA)

12. What are the different types of wireless networks used in mobile computing? (Mumbai University, December 2023, MCA)

Answers

Exercise 1- 1. a) Voice over Long-Term Evolution. 2. b) OFDM
Exercise 2- 1. False. 2. True
Exercise 3- 1. 4G. 2. OFDM
Exercise 4- 1. LTE. 2. 3G
Exercise 5- 1. LTE is a high-speed standard of 4G.
2. 4G improved data speeds and audio services with HD quality.
Exercise 6. 1. d) 3G. 2. d) SMS
Exercise 7- 1. OFDM. 2. LTE
Exercise 8- 1 – c. 2 – a. 3 – b. 4 - d
Exercise 9- 1. c) Assertion is true, but the reason is false.
2. a) Both assertion and reason are true, and the reason is the correct explanation.
Exercise 10-

M	H	F	L	M	E	**L**	**T**	**E**	T
U	O	R	W	E	R	T	Y	U	A
L	P	E	D	W	**V**	**O**	**L**	**T**	**E**
T	O	Q	R	T	Y	H	S	I	W
I	I	U	C	V	B	N	M	V	V
P	U	E	O	M	N	G	U	I	D
L	Y	N	P	L	U	U	V	S	A
E	H	C	E	K	S	N	X	I	T
X	G	Y	T	J	E	S	W	O	A
S	O	X	S	V	R	E	S	N	S

s

Exercise 11- 1. Long-Term Evolution. 2. VoLTE

Test Paper

Chapter-4
Third and Fourth Generation (3G & 4G) Networks

Time Duration: 30 Minutes **Maximum Marks: 25**

General Instructions:

1. The question paper consists of 12 questions and is divided into four sections, A, B, C and D.
2. All questions are compulsory.
3. Section A comprises MCQs, fill in the blanks and True or False carrying one marks each.
4. Section B comprises VSAQs (very short answers questions) carrying two marks each.
5. Section C comprises SAQs (short questions) carrying four marks each.
6. Section D comprises long questions carrying five marks each.

SECTION-A

Q1. Multiple choice questions: **(1*2=2)**

1. What technology in 4G networks allows voice calls with improved audio quality?

a) OFDM
b) LTE
c) VoLTE
d) GSM

2. Which feature was introduced with 3G networks?

a) HD streaming
b) Multimedia messaging
c) OFDM transmission
d) Online gaming

Q2. Fill in the blanks: **(1*2=2)**

1. _____ is the technology standard in 4G networks that offers high-speed wireless communication.
2. 3G networks introduced _____ messaging and video calling capabilities.

Q3. True or False: **(1*2=2)**

1. LTE reduces latency and handles high-capacity data demands.
2. 4G networks are less power-intensive for devices than 3G networks.

SECTION-B

Q4. Very Short answers type questions-I **(2*3=6)**

1. What are the key advantages of 4G over 3G networks?
2. Define LTE and its role in 4G networks.
3. What is the function of OFDM in mobile networks?

SECTION-C

Q5. Short answers type questions-II **(4*2=8)**

1. Compare the services and applications enabled by 3G and 4G networks.
2. Explain the challenges of implementing 3G and 4G networks.

SECTION-D

Q6. Long answers type questions **(5*1=5)**

1. Describe how the evolution from 3G to 4G has impacted mobile communication and data services.

Chapter 5 - Wireless Networks and Communication

In this chapter you will learn about:

- Definition and Characteristics of Wireless Networks
- Fixed vs. Wireless Networks
- Types of Wireless Networks (LAN, PAN, MAN)
- Wireless Communication Protocols
- Applications of Wireless Networks

Wireless networks have transformed how we communicate, access information, and interact with technology. Unlike traditional wired networks, wireless networks utilise radio waves and other wireless communication technologies to transmit data, allowing greater mobility and flexibility. This chapter explores the definition and characteristics of wireless networks, differentiates between fixed and wireless networks, examines various wireless networks, delves into communication protocols, highlights practical applications, and provides a glossary of key terms, a summary, and previous year's solved questions.

5.1 Definition and Characteristics of Wireless Networks

Definition: Wireless networks allow devices to communicate without physical cables, using radio waves or infrared signals.

- Characteristics:
- Mobility: Users can access network resources from various locations.
- Flexibility: Easy to install and configure, adaptable to changing environments.
- Scalability: Easily expandable by adding new devices without significant infrastructure changes.
- Cost-Effectiveness: Reduces the need for extensive cabling and infrastructure.

5.2 Fixed vs. Wireless Networks

- Fixed Networks: Physical cables (e.g., Ethernet) are used for connectivity; they often provide stable and high-speed connections.
- Wireless Networks: Rely on wireless signals; may have variable speed and stability but offer greater mobility.
- Comparison:
- Installation: Fixed networks require more physical labour; wireless networks can be set up quickly.
- Cost: Fixed networks can be more expensive to deploy in extensive areas due to cabling costs.
- Performance: Fixed networks generally offer more reliable performance compared to wireless.

5.3 Types of Wireless Networks (LAN, PAN, MAN, WAN)

- Wireless Local Area Network (WLAN): Covers a small area, such as a home or office; common standard is Wi-Fi.
- Wireless Personal Area Network (WPAN): Short-range network (e.g., Bluetooth); used for personal devices.
- Wireless Metropolitan Area Network (WMAN): Larger than a LAN, can cover an entire city; often used for public Wi-Fi.
- Wireless Wide Area Network (WWAN): Covers larger geographical areas; typically provided by mobile network operators.

5.4 Wireless Communication Protocols

- 802.11 (Wi-Fi): Standards for WLANs; multiple versions with varying speed and range (e.g., 802.11n, 802.11ac).
- Bluetooth: Standard for WPANs, allowing short-range device communication.
- Zigbee: Designed for low-power, low-data-rate applications, ideal for IoT devices.
- LTE (Long-Term Evolution): A standard for high-speed wireless communication for mobile phones and data terminals.

5.5 Applications of Wireless Networks

- Mobile Communication: Enabling voice and data services for smartphones and tablets.
- IoT Devices: Connecting smart appliances, wearables, and sensors for data collection and automation.
- Public Wi-Fi: Offering internet access in public spaces like cafes, airports, and libraries.
- Remote Work: Facilitating communication and collaboration among remote teams.

5.6 Glossary

- Wireless Network: A network that connects devices without physical cables.
- WLAN: Wireless Local Area Network.

• Bluetooth: A wireless technology standard for exchanging data over short distances.
• IoT: Internet of Things, referring to interconnected devices communicating via the internet.

5.7 Summary

• **Transformation of Communication:**
  o Wireless networks have revolutionised how we communicate and access information by enabling mobility and flexibility.
• **Definition of Wireless Networks:**
  o Wireless networks utilise radio waves and other technologies for data transmission, allowing devices to connect without physical cables.

Key Characteristics:
  o **Mobility:** Users can connect from various locations, enhancing convenience.
  o **Scalability:** Easily accommodate new devices without extensive infrastructure.
  o **Flexibility:** Supports diverse applications across different environments.
  o **Interference and Range:** Performance can be affected by various factors such as obstacles, distance, and electromagnetic interference.

Comparison of Fixed vs. Wireless Networks:
  o **Fixed Networks:** Typically involve wired connections; more reliable but less flexible.
• **Installation and Maintenance:** Wireless networks are generally easier to set up and maintain than wired networks.
• **Cost Implications:** Initial infrastructure costs may differ; wireless may reduce cabling costs.
• **Performance Differences:** Depending on the technology used, wireless networks may have lower speeds and reliability than wired counterparts.

Types of Wireless Networks:
  o **Local Area Network (LAN):** Covers a small geographical area (e.g., homes, offices) and is commonly implemented using Wi-Fi.
• **Personal Area Network (PAN):** This is very short-range communication, typically using Bluetooth technology to connect personal devices.
• **Metropolitan Area Network (MAN):** This network connects multiple LANs within a city, supporting community services and connectivity.
• **Wide Area Network (WAN):** Extends over large geographical distances, facilitating global connectivity.
• IEEE 802.11 (Wi-Fi) is the major standard for wireless LANs, with various specifications (e.g., 802.11ac, 802.11ax).
• **Bluetooth:** Short-range communication protocol widely used for connecting peripherals and personal devices.
• **Zigbee:** A protocol for low-power, low-data-rate applications, often used in IoT environments.
• NFC (near-Field Communication) allows short-range communication, and it is commonly used in mobile payments and access control.
• **Comparison:** Each protocol has specific strengths and weaknesses, catering to different applications and use cases.

Applications of Wireless Networks:
• **Home Networking:** Utilization of Wi-Fi for internet access and smart home devices.
• **Mobile Communication**: Dependency of smartphones and tablets on wireless connectivity for functionality.
• **Healthcare:** Deployment of wireless monitoring systems and telemedicine for patient care.
• **Transportation:** Implementation of V2X communication systems and GPS tracking for vehicles.
• **Industrial Automation:** Adoption of wireless IoT solutions in manufacturing, logistics, and supply chain management.

5.8 Previous Year Solved Question

Question: What are wireless networks, and how do they differ from wired networks? (Anna University, July 2022, MCA)
Answer: Wireless networks are communication systems that transmit data using radio waves or infrared signals, allowing devices to connect without physical cables. The key differences between wireless and wired networks include:
• **Mobility:** Wireless networks offer greater mobility, enabling users to connect from various locations. In contrast, wired networks require physical connections.
• **Installation:** Wireless networks are generally easier to install and maintain, as they do not require extensive cabling.

• **Cost:** Initial costs for wireless infrastructure may be lower due to the absence of cabling; however, performance might vary based on distance and interference.
• **Performance:** Wired networks usually provide higher speeds and lower latency than wireless networks, which may be affected by environmental factors.

Exercises

Exercise 1 – Multiple Choice Questions

1. What is IoT?
a) A wireless standard for LAN communication
b) Internet of Things, referring to interconnected devices
c) A protocol for mobile payments
d) A short-range communication standard

2. Which wireless technology is primarily used for connecting personal devices over short distances?
(a) WLAN
(b) NFC
(c) Bluetooth
(d) Wi-Fi

Exercise 2 – True/False

1. Bluetooth is a wireless technology used for short-range communication between devices.
2. WANs are restricted to small geographical areas, like homes or offices.

Exercise 3 – Fill in the blanks

1. Wireless networks utilize _____ waves for data transmission.
2. NFC technology is often used for _____ payments.

Exercise 4- Fill in the blanks with two options

1. WLAN covers a _____ (small/large) geographical area, commonly used in homes and offices.
2. Bluetooth is designed for _____ (long-range/short-range) communication between personal devices.

Exercise 5- Rearrange the sentence

1. Standard / for / Wi-Fi / IEEE 802.11 / the / wireless LANs / is.
2. Flexibility / connect / locations / Users / from / various / can.

Exercise 6- Choose the Odd One Out

1. a) LAN
b) MAN
c) WLAN
d) WAN
2. a) Bluetooth
b) Wi-Fi
c) NFC
d) Ethernet

Exercise 7- Jumble words

1. FNC (Hint: Used in mobile payments)
2. TLEBOUHTO (Hint: A wireless technology for short distances)

Exercise 8- Match case

1. IoT
2. NFC
3. Bluetooth
4. WLAN

a) Short-range communication for personal devices

b) Communication between interconnected devices
c) Used for mobile payments and access control
d) Wireless Local Area Network

Exercise 9- Assertion – Reason

1. **Assertion:** Bluetooth is used in PANs for short-range communication.
Reason: Bluetooth technology allows long-distance connections.
a) Both assertion and reason are true, and the reason is the correct explanation.
b) Both assertion and reason are true, but the reason is not the correct explanation.
c) Assertion is true, but the reason is false.
d) Both assertion and reason are false.
2. **Assertion:** WLANs are easier to set up than wired networks.
Reason: WLANs require less cabling infrastructure.
a) Both assertion and reason are true, and the reason is the correct explanation.
b) Both assertion and reason are true, but the reason is not the correct explanation.
c) Assertion is true, but the reason is false.
d) Both assertion and reason are false.

Exercise 10- Read the questions below and find the appropriate word in the provided grid.

1. Identify the technology that allows devices to communicate without physical cables.
2. Find the term referring to a personal area network standard.

M	H	F	L	B	L	U	E	T	O
I	O	T	Y	F	G	E	D	Y	A
P	N	E	F	C	T	U	O	U	X
T	O	Q	R	T	Y	H	S	I	W
I	I	W	A	N	B	N	M	V	V
P	L	A	N	M	N	G	U	I	D
L	B	L	E	U	U	U	V	S	A
E	N	C	E	K	S	N	X	I	T
X	G	Y	T	J	E	S	W	O	A
S	O	X	S	V	R	E	S	N	S

Exercise 11- One- word

1. What wireless technology is commonly used for short-range personal devices?
2. Which technology allows mobile payments and access control?

Exercise 12- Small Answers

1. Explain the role of WLANs in home networking.
2. What are the key advantages of wireless networks over wired networks?

Exercise 13- Long Answers

1. Describe the key characteristics of wireless networks and the differences between LAN, PAN, MAN, and WAN.
2. What are the main advantages and challenges of implementing wireless networks in various industries?

Exercise 14- Previous Years Unsolved Questions

1. Explain the concept of near-field communication (NFC) in mobile computing and its applications. (Anna University, July 2022, MCA)
2. Discuss the role of mobile computing in disaster management and emergency response. (IGNOU, December 2021, MCA)
3. What is mobile ad hoc networking (MANET)? How does it differ from traditional networks? (Anna University, June 2022, MCA)

4. Explain the significance of mobile computing in the context of smart cities. (Mumbai University, December 2023, MCA)
5. How does mobile computing support e-commerce and mobile payments? Provide examples. (IGNOU, December 2021, MCA)
6. Write a short note on wearable devices in the context of mobile computing. (Anna University, July 2022, MCA)
7. Discuss the role of mobile computing in the Internet of Things (IoT) ecosystem. (Anna University, June 2022, MCA)
8. What is the privacy concerns associated with location-based services in mobile computing? (IGNOU, December 2021, MCA)
9. Explain the difference between mobile web applications and native mobile applications. (Anna University, July 2022, MCA)
10. How do mobile operating systems (like Android and iOS) manage multitasking? (Mumbai University, December 2023, MCA)
11. What is the role of GPS in mobile computing? Explain with an example. (IGNOU, December 2021, MCA)
12. Discuss the key trends in mobile app development for mobile computing. (Anna University, June 2022, MCA)

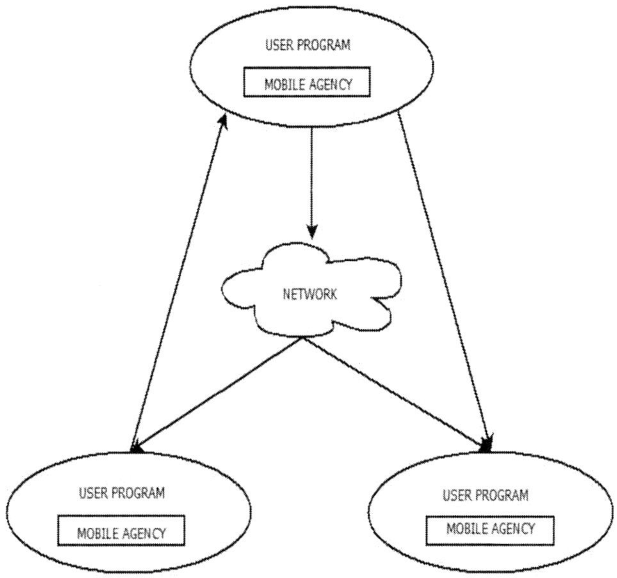

Answers

Exercise 1- 1. b) Internet of Things, referring to interconnected devices. 2.c) Bluetooth
Exercise 2- 1. True. 2. False
Exercise 3- 1. Radio. 2. mobile
Exercise 4- 1. Small. 2. short-range
Exercise 5- 1. IEEE 802.11 is the standard for wireless LANs. 2. Users can connect from various locations.
Exercise 6. 1. c) WLAN. 2. d) Ethernet
Exercise 7- 1. NFC. 2. Bluetooth
Exercise 8- 1 – b. 2 – c. 3 – a. 4 - d
Exercise 9- 1. c) Assertion is true, but the reason is false.
2. a) Both assertion and reason are true, and the reason is the correct explanation.
Exercise 10-

B	**L**	**U**	**E**	**T**	**O**	**O**	**T**	**H**	O
I	**O**	**T**	Y	F	G	E	D	Y	A
P	N	E	F	C	T	U	O	U	X
T	O	Q	R	T	Y	H	S	I	W
I	I	W	A	N	B	N	M	V	V
P	L	A	N	M	N	G	U	I	D
L	B	L	E	U	U	U	V	S	A
E	N	C	E	K	S	N	X	I	T
X	G	Y	T	J	E	S	W	O	A
S	O	X	S	V	R	E	S	N	S

Exercise 11- 1. Bluetooth. 2. NFC

Test Paper

Chapter-5
Wireless Networks and Communication

Time Duration: 30 Minutes **Maximum Marks: 25**

General Instructions:

1. The question paper consists of 12 questions and is divided into four sections, A, B, C and D.
2. All questions are compulsory.
3. Section A comprises MCQs, fill in the blanks and True or False carrying one marks each.
4. Section B comprises VSAQs (very short answers questions) carrying two marks each.
5. Section C comprises SAQs (short questions) carrying four marks each.
6. Section D comprises long questions carrying five marks each.

SECTION-A

Q1. Multiple choice questions: **(1*2=2)**

1. Which technology is commonly used for short-range communication between personal devices?
   a) Wi-Fi
   b) Bluetooth
   c) Zigbee
   d) NFC

2. What type of network connects multiple LANs within a city?
   a) PAN
   b) WLAN
   c) MAN
   d) WAN

Q2. Fill in the blanks: **(1*2=2)**

1. Wireless networks rely on _____ waves for data transmission.
2. _____ is a major standard for wireless LANs, often used for internet access.

Q3. True or False: **(1*2=2)**

1. Wireless networks offer greater reliability than fixed networks.
2. Bluetooth is commonly used for connecting peripherals and personal devices over short distances.

SECTION-B

Q4. Very Short answers type questions-I **(2*3=6)**

1. What is the key difference between wireless and fixed networks?
2. Define a Personal Area Network (PAN) and give an example of its application.
3. How do wireless networks enable greater flexibility compared to wired networks?

SECTION-C

Q5. Short answers type questions-II **(4*2=8)**

1. Explain the different types of wireless networks and their applications.
2. Discuss the advantages and disadvantages of wireless networks compared to fixed networks.

SECTION-D

Q6. Long answers type questions **(5*1=5)**

1. Describe the various protocols used in wireless networks, including Bluetooth, Zigbee, and NFC, and compare their use cases and strengths.

Chapter 6 - Modulation Techniques in Mobile Communication

In this chapter you will learn about:

- What is Modulation?
- Minimum Shift Keying (MSK) Modulation
- Spread Spectrum Techniques
- Frequency and Phase Modulation in Mobile Networks
- Applications of Modulation in Mobile Systems

Modulation is a fundamental technique in communication systems that enables data transmission over various media, particularly in mobile communication. It involves altering the properties of a carrier signal—such as its amplitude, frequency, or phase—to encode information. Modulation is essential for effectively using the available bandwidth, enhancing signal quality, and minimising interference and noise. This chapter explores different modulation techniques, including Minimum Shift Keying (MSK), spread spectrum methods, and the roles of frequency and phase modulation in mobile networks. Additionally, it examines the applications of these modulation techniques in modern mobile systems.

6.1 What is Modulation?

Modulation is the process of varying a carrier signal by the information signal to facilitate effective transmission over communication channels. The primary purposes of modulation include:

- **Bandwidth Utilization:** Modulation allows transmitting multiple signals over the same channel without interference, optimising available bandwidth.
- **Signal Resilience:** Modulated signals are less susceptible to noise and interference, improving overall transmission quality.
- **Distance Coverage**: Modulation techniques enable signals to travel longer distances, particularly important for mobile communication systems operating over vast geographical areas.

There are two main types of modulation:

- **Analog Modulation:** Techniques that continuously vary the carrier signal, such as Amplitude Modulation (AM) and Frequency Modulation (FM).
- **Digital Modulation:** Techniques that encode digital data into specific signal changes, including Phase Shift Keying (PSK) and Frequency Shift Keying (FSK).

6.2 Minimum Shift Keying (MSK) Modulation

Minimum Shift Keying (MSK) is a type of continuous-phase frequency shift keying where the frequency of the carrier signal is varied in small, discrete steps. The following features characterise MSK:

- **Continuous Phase:** The signal's phase changes continuously, minimizing sudden jumps that could cause spectral spreading. This characteristic results in a cleaner signal with reduced sideband power.
- **Spectral Efficiency:** MSK has a higher spectral efficiency than other modulation techniques, allowing it to transmit data within a smaller bandwidth while maintaining good signal quality.
- **Low Error Rates**: Due to its continuous phase characteristics, MSK experiences lower error rates in noisy environments, making it suitable for mobile communication systems.MSK is widely used in the Global System for Mobile Communications (GSM) and other mobile standards, as it effectively balances performance and bandwidth efficiency.

6.3 Spread Spectrum Techniques

Spread spectrum techniques spread a signal across a wide frequency range, providing increased resistance to interference and security. There are two primary types of spread spectrum techniques:

- **Frequency Hopping Spread Spectrum (FHSS):** In this technique, the carrier frequency rapidly changes according to a predefined sequence, hopping from one frequency to another within the available bandwidth. This reduces the likelihood of interference since the signal is not continuously transmitted on a single frequency.
- **Direct Sequence Spread Spectrum (DSSS):** DSSS spreads the signal by multiplying it with a pseudo-random noise (PN) sequence, which increases the signal's bandwidth. This method enhances resistance to jamming and interference, as the original signal can be recovered only by synchronizing with the PN sequence.

Advantages of Spread Spectrum Techniques:

- **Robustness:** Spread spectrum signals are more resistant to noise and interference, ensuring reliable communication even in challenging environments.

- **Security:** The spreading process provides security, making it difficult for unauthorized users to intercept or decode the transmitted signals.
- **Multiple Accesses:** Techniques like Code Division Multiple Access (CDMA) utilize spread spectrum methods to allow multiple users to share the same frequency band without interference.

6.4 Frequency and Phase Modulation in Mobile Networks

In mobile networks, frequency and phase modulation play crucial roles in ensuring effective data transmission:

- **Frequency Modulation (FM)**: In FM, the frequency of the carrier signal varies according to the amplitude of the input signal. FM is widely used in mobile communications, particularly for transmitting audio signals, due to its resistance to noise and interference. The modulation index determines the extent of frequency variation and affects the bandwidth requirements.
- **Phase Modulation (PM)**: PM alters the phase of the carrier signal based on the input data. It is resilient to noise and can be effectively used in digital modulation schemes, such as Phase Shift Keying (PSK). PSK encodes data by changing the phase of the carrier signal, making it efficient for high-speed data transmission.

Both FM and PM are integral to the design of modern mobile communication systems, contributing to the robustness and efficiency of data transmission.

6.5 Applications of Modulation in Mobile Systems

Modulation techniques are essential for various applications in mobile systems:

- **Voice Communication:** Modulation enables the effective transmission of voice signals over mobile networks, ensuring conversation clarity and reliability.
- **Data Transmission:** Mobile internet services rely on modulation techniques to transmit data packets efficiently, supporting activities like browsing, streaming, and online gaming.
- **Broadcasting:** Modulation is used in television and radio broadcasting to transmit audio and video signals over long distances, allowing for widespread media distribution.
- **Satellite Communication:** Modulation techniques are critical for encoding and transmitting signals to and from satellites, facilitating global communication.
- **Remote Sensing:** Environmental monitoring and data collection applications rely on modulation to transmit information from remote sensors to data centres for analysis.

6.6 Glossary

- **Modulation:** The process of varying a carrier signal to encode data for transmission.
- **Carrier Signal:** A waveform used to carry information-bearing signals.
- **Spectral Efficiency:** A measure of how efficiently a modulation scheme uses available bandwidth.
- **Frequency Hopping:** A technique rapidly changing the transmission frequency to reduce interference.
- **Direct Sequence Spread Spectrum:** A method of spreading a signal by multiplying it with a pseudo-random noise sequence.

6.7 Summary

- **Modulation Overview:**
  - Modulation is varying a carrier signal to transmit data over communication channels.
  - Key purposes include optimising bandwidth utilisation, enhancing signal resilience, and extending transmission distances.

Types of Modulation:

- **Analog Modulation:** Techniques like Amplitude Modulation (AM) and Frequency Modulation (FM) vary the carrier signal continuously.
- **Digital Modulation:** Techniques such as Phase Shift Keying (PSK) and Frequency Shift Keying (FSK) encode digital data into specific signal changes.

Minimum Shift Keying (MSK):

- A type of continuous-phase frequency shift keying with small frequency shifts.
- Characteristics include continuous phase, high spectral efficiency, and low error rates.
- Commonly used in GSM and other mobile standards.

Spread Spectrum Techniques:

Spread spectrum methods spread a signal over a wide frequency range, increasing resistance to interference and enhancing security.

- **Frequency Hopping Spread Spectrum (FHSS):** Rapidly changes frequencies to avoid interference.

• **Direct Sequence Spread Spectrum (DSSS):** Spreads signals by multiplying them with a pseudo-random noise sequence.

Frequency and Phase Modulation:
• **Frequency Modulation (FM):** Varies the carrier frequency based on the input signal amplitude; used for audio transmission.
• **Phase Modulation (PM):** Alters the phase of the carrier signal based on input data; effective for high-speed data transmission.

Applications of Modulation:
• Voice communication in mobile networks.
• Data transmission for mobile internet services.
• Broadcasting audio and video signals.
• Satellite communication for global connectivity.
• Remote sensing for environmental monitoring.

Key Terminology:
• **Carrier Signal:** A waveform used to carry information.
• **Spectral Efficiency:** Efficiency of a modulation scheme in utilizing bandwidth.
• **Frequency Hopping**: Technique that rapidly changes transmission frequency.
• **Direct Sequence Spread Spectrum (DSSS):** Spreading a signal by multiplying it with a noise sequence.

6.8 Previous Year Solved Question

Question: Explain the concept of modulation in mobile communication. Discuss its significance and the types of modulation techniques used in modern communication systems. (IGNOU, December 2021, MCA)
Answer: Modulation is the process of varying one or more characteristics of a carrier signal—such as amplitude, frequency, or phase—according to the information signal. This technique is crucial in mobile communication because it allows for efficient data transmission over various communication channels while optimising bandwidth and enhancing signal quality.

The significance of modulation in mobile communication includes:
o **Bandwidth Optimization:** By modulating signals, multiple channels can coexist within the same frequency range without interference, allowing for more efficient use of the available spectrum.
o **Improved Signal Quality:** Modulated signals are more resistant to noise and interference, ensuring reliable communication even in adverse conditions.
o **Extended Range:** Modulation enables signals to be transmitted over long distances, making it possible for mobile devices to communicate effectively across large areas.

The primary types of modulation techniques used in modern communication systems include:
o Analog Modulation: Techniques such as Amplitude Modulation (AM) and Frequency Modulation (FM) are used primarily in traditional radio and television broadcasting.
o Digital Modulation: Techniques like Phase Shift Keying (PSK), Frequency Shift Keying (FSK), and Minimum Shift Keying (MSK) are used for digital data transmission, enabling high-speed data transfer in mobile networks. Digital modulation allows for better error detection and correction, essential for maintaining the integrity of the transmitted data.

Exercises

Exercise 1 – Multiple Choice Questions

1. What is the purpose of Frequency Hopping Spread Spectrum (FHSS)?

a) To increase the carrier signal strength
b) To rapidly change frequencies and reduce interference
c) To continuously phase-shift the carrier signal
d) To encode data using pseudo-random noise

2. Which modulation technique is commonly used for audio transmission?

a) Phase Modulation (PM)
b) Frequency Modulation (FM)
c) Direct Sequence Spread Spectrum (DSSS)
d) Minimum Shift Keying (MSK)

Exercise 2 – True/False

1. Spectral efficiency measures how efficiently a modulation scheme uses bandwidth.
2. Phase Modulation (PM) varies the carrier signal frequency based on input data.

Exercise 3 – Fill in the blanks

1. _____ is a modulation technique where the transmission frequency changes rapidly to avoid interference.
2. In _____ Modulation, the amplitude of the input signal affects the carrier frequency.

Exercise 4- Fill in the blanks with two options

1. Minimum Shift Keying (MSK) is commonly used in _____ (GSM/FHSS) for mobile communication.
2. _____ (Analog/Digital) modulation techniques include PSK and FSK to encode digital data.

Exercise 5- Rearrange the sentence

1. Spreads / spectrum / signal / techniques / range / wide / Spread / over / a / frequency.
2. Process / varying / signal / Modulation / carrier / is / data / for / the / of / transmission.

Exercise 6- Choose the Odd One Out

1. a) Amplitude Modulation (AM)
b) Frequency Modulation (FM)
c) Phase Modulation (PM)
d) Minimum Shift Keying (MSK)
2. a) DSSS
b) FHSS
c) Spectral Efficiency
d) Direct Sequence

Exercise 7- Jumble words

1. SQSD (Hint: A spread spectrum technique using a noise sequence)
2. ROEMLUTADINO (Hint: The process of varying a signal to transmit data)

Exercise 8- Match case

1. Modulation
2. Frequency Hopping (FHSS)
3. Carrier Signal
4. Direct Sequence Spread Spectrum (DSSS)

a) Rapidly changing transmission frequency
b) The waveform used to carry data signals
c) Process of varying a carrier signal
d) Spreading signals with a noise sequence

Exercise 9- Assertion – Reason

1. **Assertion:** MSK modulation is known for high spectral efficiency.
Reason: MSK involves large frequency shifts in its modulation technique.
a) Both assertion and reason are true, and the reason is the correct explanation.
b) Both assertion and reason are true, but the reason is not the correct explanation.
c) Assertion is true, but the reason is false.
d) Both assertion and reason are false.

2. **Assertion:** Spread spectrum techniques increase resistance to interference.
Reason: Spread spectrum methods use a narrow frequency range for data transmission.
a) Both assertion and reason are true, and the reason is the correct explanation.
b) Both assertion and reason are true, but the reason is not the correct explanation.
c) Assertion is true, but the reason is false.
d) Both assertion and reason are false.

Exercise 10- Read the questions below and find the appropriate word in the provided grid.

1. Identify the modulation technique that spreads a signal using a noise sequence.
2. Find the technique that rapidly switches frequencies to avoid interference.

I	M	D	F	R	E	Q	S	P	A
P	S	P	C	R	H	H	F	I	X
T	O	Q	R	T	K	N	Y	I	W
I	I	W	A	S	B	E	M	F	V
P	L	A	N	Q	N	G	T	I	D
L	B	L	E	C	U	U	V	S	A
E	N	C	F	K	S	N	X	I	T
X	G	Y	T	J	E	S	W	O	A
S	O	X	S	V	R	E	S	N	S

Exercise 11- One- word

1. What modulation technique spreads a signal using a noise sequence?
2. Which modulation method rapidly changes transmission frequency to avoid interference?

Exercise 12- Small Answers

1. What are the key advantages of spread spectrum techniques?
2. Explain the role of carrier signals in communication.

Exercise 13- Long Answers

1. Describe the differences between Analog and Digital modulation, providing examples of each.
2. How do modulation techniques impact the performance of mobile communication systems?

Exercise 14- Previous Years Unsolved Questions

1. How do push notifications work in mobile computing? What are the benefits and challenges? (Anna University, July 2022, MCA)
2. Explain the challenges of mobile application testing and quality assurance. (Mumbai University, December 2023, MCA)
3. What is the role of mobile computing in social networking? (IGNOU, December 2021, MCA)
4. Describe the process of app store optimization for mobile applications. (Anna University, June 2022, MCA)
5. How does mobile computing support real-time data processing? (Anna University, July 2022, MCA)

6. Discuss the ethical issues surrounding mobile app data collection. (IGNOU, December 2021, MCA)
7. What is the role of artificial intelligence in enhancing mobile computing applications? (Mumbai University, December 2023, MCA)
8. Explain the role of 5G in enabling advanced mobile computing solutions. (Anna University, June 2022, MCA)

Answers

Exercise 1- 1. b) To rapidly change frequencies and reduce interference 2. b) Frequency Modulation (FM)
Exercise 2- 1. True. 2. False
Exercise 3- 1. Frequency Hopping. 2. Frequency Modulation
Exercise 4- 1. GSM. 2. Digital
Exercise 5- 1. Spread spectrum techniques spread a signal over a wide frequency range.
2. Modulation is the process of varying a carrier signal for data transmission.
Exercise 6. 1. d) Minimum Shift Keying (MSK). 2. c) Spectral Efficiency
Exercise 7- 1. DSSS. 2.Modulation
Exercise 8- 1 – c. 2 – a. 3 – b. 4 - d
Exercise 9- 1. c) Assertion is true, but the reason is false. 2. c) Assertion is true, but the reason is false.
Exercise 10-

I	M	D	F	R	**D**	S	S	S	A
P	S	P	C	R	H	H	F	I	X
T	O	Q	R	T	K	N	Y	I	W
I	I	**F**	A	S	B	E	M	F	V
P	L	**H**	N	Q	N	G	T	I	D
L	B	S	E	C	U	U	V	S	A
E	N	S	F	K	S	N	X	I	T
X	G	Y	T	J	E	S	W	O	A
S	O	X	S	V	R	E	S	N	S

Exercise 11- 1. DSSS. 2. FHSS

Test Paper

Chapter-6
Modulation Techniques in Mobile Communication

Time Duration: 30 Minutes **Maximum Marks: 25**

General Instructions:

1. The question paper consists of 12 questions and is divided into four sections, A, B, C and D.
2. All questions are compulsory.
3. Section A comprises MCQs, fill in the blanks and True or False carrying one marks each.
4. Section B comprises VSAQs (very short answers questions) carrying two marks each.
5. Section C comprises SAQs (short questions) carrying four marks each.
6. Section D comprises long questions carrying five marks each.

SECTION-A

Q1. Multiple choice questions: **(1*2=2)**

1. Which modulation technique varies the carrier signal's frequency based on the input signal amplitude?

a) Phase Modulation (PM)
b) Frequency Modulation (FM)
c) Amplitude Modulation (AM)
d) Frequency Shift Keying (FSK)

2. What is the primary purpose of Frequency Hopping Spread Spectrum (FHSS)?

a) Encode digital data
b) Reduce interference
c) Improve spectral efficiency
d) Enhance audio quality

Q2. Fill in the blanks: **(1*2=2)**

1. _____ Modulation is effective for high-speed data transmission by altering the phase of the carrier signal.
2. A _____ signal is a waveform used to carry information-bearing signals.

Q3. True or False: **(1*2=2)**

1. Direct Sequence Spread Spectrum (DSSS) multiplies a signal with a pseudo-random noise sequence.
2. Spectral efficiency measures how quickly a signal changes frequency to avoid interference.

SECTION-B

Q4. Very Short answers type questions-I **(2*3=6)**

1. What is modulation, and why is it important in communication systems?
2. Define MSK and mention one of its characteristics.
3. What is the difference between analog and digital modulation techniques?

SECTION-C

Q5. Short answers type questions-II **(4*2=8)**

1. Explain the role of spread spectrum techniques in enhancing signal security and interference resistance.
2. Describe the differences between Frequency Modulation (FM) and Phase Modulation (PM).

SECTION-D

Q6. Long answers type questions **(5*1=5)**

1. Discuss the applications of modulation in different communication systems and explain how spectral efficiency impacts transmission.

Chapter 7 - Bluetooth and Short-Range Wireless Technologies

In this chapter you will learn about:

- Overview of Bluetooth Technology
- Comparison of Bluetooth with Other Short-Range Technologies
- Bluetooth Profiles and Applications
- Advantages and Limitations of Bluetooth

Bluetooth is a widely used wireless technology for short-range communication between electronic devices. It enables devices to connect and exchange data without cables, making it highly popular in personal area networks (PAN). Developed in the 1990s by Ericsson, Bluetooth has evolved through multiple versions, enhancing speed, range, and energy efficiency. It powers various applications, from wireless audio streaming and file sharing to health monitoring and home automation. Bluetooth is valued for its ease of use, low power consumption, and compatibility across various devices, including smart phones, laptops, smartwatches, and IoT devices.

7.1 Overview of Bluetooth Technology

Bluetooth operates on the 2.4 GHz ISM (Industrial, Scientific, and Medical) frequency band, making it suitable for short-range communication, usually within 10 metres. Devices use radio waves to communicate, and Bluetooth supports point-to-point (between two devices) and multipoint connections (between multiple devices). Over the years, Bluetooth technology has improved range and speed, leading to new versions like Bluetooth Low Energy (BLE), which consumes minimal power and is ideal for IoT and fitness devices. Its versatility has made Bluetooth a key technology for connecting personal devices and building smart ecosystems.

7.2 Bluetooth Protocol Stack and Architecture

Bluetooth communication relies on a layered protocol stack, ensuring smooth and secure data transfer. Here's an overview of the layers:

• **Radio Layer:** Handles physical transmission using radio waves.
• **Baseband Layer:** Manages the formation of connections, addressing, and error control.
• **Link Manager Protocol (LMP):** Takes care of pairing, authentication, and encryption to secure communication.
• **Logical Link Control and Adaptation Protocol (L2CAP):** Manages data packet segmentation and flow control.
• **Service Discovery Protocol (SDP):** Enables devices to discover the services other Bluetooth devices offer.

This structure ensures compatibility, low energy consumption, and reliable data exchange across devices.

7.3 Comparison of Bluetooth with Other Short-Range Technologies

Bluetooth is often compared with other wireless technologies that offer short-range communication. Here's a quick comparison:

Technology	Range	Speed	Best Use Cases	Power Consumption
Bluetooth	Up to 10 meters	1–2 Mbps	Audio devices, fitness trackers, file sharing	Low
Wi-Fi	30–50 meters	Up to 1 Gbps	Internet access, video streaming	High
NFC	4–10 cm	424 kbps	Contactless payments, identity verification	Very low
Zigbee	10–100 meters	250 kbps	Smart home, industrial IoT devices	Very low

Bluetooth stands out for its low power consumption, making it ideal for portable and wearable devices, while Wi-Fi is better suited for high-speed internet access over larger areas.

7.4 Bluetooth Profiles and Applications

Bluetooth profiles are predefined sets of rules that ensure devices can communicate adequately. Below are some widely used profiles:

• **HFP (Hands-Free Profile):** Facilitates voice calls via Bluetooth in cars or headsets.
• **A2DP (Advanced Audio Distribution Profile):** Enables high-quality audio streaming from phones to speakers or earphones.

- **HID (Human Interface Device):** Supports input devices like Bluetooth keyboards, mice, and gaming controllers.
- **PAN (Personal Area Networking Profile):** Allows devices to share internet connections.

Applications of Bluetooth Technology:

- **Wireless Audio:** Bluetooth headphones, earphones, and speakers are used for music streaming and calls.
- **Fitness Tracking:** Wearable devices like smart watches connect to smartphones via Bluetooth to sync health data.
- **File Transfer:** Bluetooth enables quick sharing of files between smartphones and laptops.
- **Home Automation:** Smart lights and appliances use Bluetooth for localized control.

7.5 Advantages and Limitations of Bluetooth

Advantages

- **Wireless Convenience:** Eliminates the hassle of connecting cables between devices.
- **Low Power Usage:** Ideal for battery-operated devices such as fitness bands and smartwatches.
- **Cost-Effective:** Bluetooth modules are inexpensive, making the technology affordable for manufacturers.
- **Interoperability:** Devices from different brands can communicate smoothly using Bluetooth standards.

Limitations

- **Limited Range:** Bluetooth generally works within 10 metres, restricting long-distance communication.
- **Interference Issues:** May experience disruptions when multiple devices operate on the 2.4 GHz frequency band.
- **Lower Data Speeds:** Compared to Wi-Fi, Bluetooth has lower data transfer speeds, limiting its use for large file transfers.
- **Security Concerns:** Bluetooth can be vulnerable to hacking attempts if devices are not adequately secured during pairing.

7.6 Glossary

- Bluetooth Protocol Stack: A set of protocols governing Bluetooth devices' communication.
- PAN (Personal Area Network): A network that connects personal devices within a short range.
- NFC (Near Field Communication): A short-range communication technology for contactless transactions.
- HFP (Hands-Free Profile): A Bluetooth profile for voice calls in vehicles or headsets.
- LMP (Link Manager Protocol): A protocol layer that handles encryption and secure communication in Bluetooth.

7.7 Summary

- Bluetooth Technology: This technology enables short-range wireless communication, typically up to 10 meters, using the 2.4 GHz band.
- Protocol Stack: Ensures secure and smooth communication with LMP, L2CAP, and SDP layers.
- Comparison: Bluetooth is ideal for low-power tasks, unlike Wi-Fi, which offers higher speeds but consumes more energy.
- Profiles and Applications: Supports voice calls (HFP), audio streaming (A2DP), and device input (HID). Used in wireless audio, fitness trackers, home automation, and file sharing.
- Advantages: Offers wireless convenience, low power consumption, interoperability, and affordability.
- Limitations: Limited range, lower speeds, interference risks, and potential security vulnerabilities.
- Conclusion: Bluetooth remains essential for personal devices and IoT ecosystems due to its versatility and energy efficiency.

7.8 Previous Year Solved Question

Question: Explain the Bluetooth protocol stack and architecture. How do its layers work together to enable smooth communication between devices? (Anna University, June 2022, MCA)

Answer: The **Bluetooth protocol stack and architecture** ensure efficient, secure, and low-power communication between Bluetooth-enabled devices. It consists of several layers, each performing specific functions necessary for smooth data transfer. Here's a breakdown of the key layers and their roles:

1. Radio Layer:

o The lowest layer is responsible for the physical transmission of data over radio frequencies (2.4 GHz).
o It defines modulation techniques and determines transmission power levels for stable communication.

2. Baseband Layer:

o This layer handles link establishment between devices and controls data packets.
o It manages physical connections, packet timing, error correction, and the device addressing system.
o It enables both synchronous (for audio) and asynchronous data transmission modes.

3. Link Manager Protocol (LMP):

o The LMP layer handles pairing, authentication, and encryption, ensuring secure connections.
o It sets up and manages link parameters, such as the power-saving mode and connection states (active or idle).
o This layer is essential for preventing unauthorised access during communication.

4. Logical Link Control and Adaptation Protocol (L2CAP):

o The L2CAP manages data segmentation and reassembly, ensuring smooth transmission even for larger data packets.
o It provides flow control to prevent data loss by regulating the rate at which devices exchange information.
o This layer supports higher-level protocols, making Bluetooth suitable for file transfers and audio streaming.

5. Service Discovery Protocol (SDP):

o The SDP allows devices to identify available services provided by other Bluetooth devices in the network.
o For example, when a Smartphone connects to a Bluetooth speaker, SDP helps the phone detect the audio playback service on the speaker.

How the Layers Work Together?

When two Bluetooth devices connect, the process begins at the **Radio layer**, establishing the physical link. The **Baseband layer** takes over to manage connections and data exchange. During the initial connection, the **Link Manager Protocol (LMP)** ensures the communication is secure through pairing and encryption. As data is transmitted, the **L2CAP layer** breaks it into smaller packets and ensures error-free transmission by controlling the data flow. Finally, the **Service Discovery Protocol (SDP)** helps devices discover the services they can use, such as audio streaming or file sharing.

These layers ensure that Bluetooth devices can connect securely, exchange data efficiently, and operate with low power consumption, making Bluetooth a versatile technology for a wide range of applications.

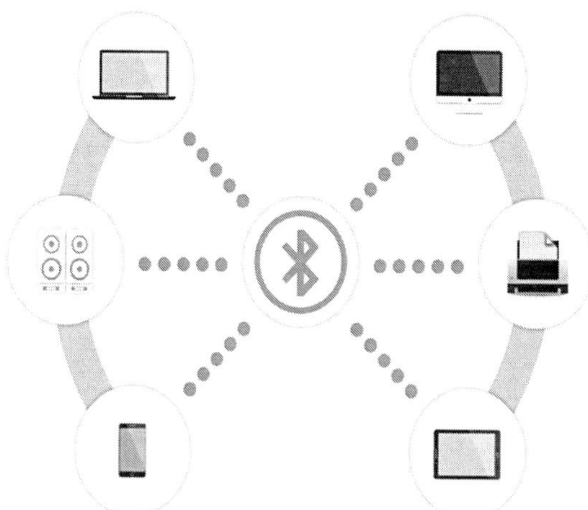

Exercises

Exercise 1 – Multiple Choice Questions

1. Which Bluetooth profile is used for voice calls in vehicles and headsets?

a) A2DP
b) HFP
c) HID
d) LMP

2. Which technology is ideal for contactless transactions?

a) Wi-Fi
b) Bluetooth
c) NFC
d) PAN

Exercise 2 – True/False

1. Bluetooth operates in the 2.4 GHz frequency band.
2. LMP is responsible for audio streaming in Bluetooth.

Exercise 3 – Fill in the blanks

1. _____ Technology supports contactless transactions through short-range communication.
2. A Bluetooth _____ stack ensures secure communication with protocol layers like LMP.

Exercise 4- Fill in the blanks with two options

1. Bluetooth is used for _____ (low-power/high-speed) tasks compared to Wi-Fi.
2. HFP is a profile for _____ (audio streaming/voice calls).

Exercise 5- Rearrange the sentence

1. Bluetooth / for / is / Low-power / tasks / suitable.
2. Protocol / secure / communication / the / ensures / stack.

Exercise 6- Choose the Odd One Out

1. a) Bluetooth
b) NFC
c) LMP
d) Wi-Fi
2. a) HFP
b) A2DP
c) PAN
d) HID

Exercise 7- Jumble words

1. FHP (Hint: Bluetooth profile for voice calls)
2. CLBMUEOT (Hint: A short-range communication technology)

Exercise 8- Match case

1. Bluetooth Protocol Stack
2. PAN
3. NFC
4. HFP

a) Technology used for contactless payments
b) A network connecting personal devices
c) Governs how Bluetooth devices communicate

d) Bluetooth profile for voice calls

Exercise 9- Assertion – Reason

1. **Assertion:** Bluetooth offers low power consumption for personal devices.

Reason: Bluetooth consumes more power than Wi-Fi for similar tasks.

a) Both assertion and reason are true, and the reason is the correct explanation.
b) Both assertion and reason are true, but the reason is not the correct explanation.
c) Assertion is true, but the reason is false.
d) Both assertion and reason are false.

2. **Assertion:** Bluetooth Protocol Stack ensures secure communication.

Reason: LMP manages encryption and secure communication.

a) Both assertion and reason are true, and the reason is the correct explanation.
b) Both assertion and reason are true, but the reason is not the correct explanation.
c) Assertion is true, but the reason is false.
d) Both assertion and reason are false.

Exercise 10- Read the questions below and find the appropriate word in the provided grid.

1. Find the Bluetooth profile used for voice calls in vehicles.
2. Identify the protocol that manages encryption in Bluetooth communication.

M	H	F	L	P	H	F	G	Q	T
I	N	C	N	R	A	S	D	I	A
H	L	P	C	F	R	H	L	P	X
T	O	Q	R	T	K	N	Y	I	W
I	I	W	A	N	B	N	M	F	V
P	L	A	N	Q	N	G	T	I	D
L	B	L	E	C	U	U	V	S	A
E	N	C	F	K	S	N	X	I	T
X	G	Y	T	J	E	S	W	O	A
S	O	X	S	V	R	E	S	N	S

Exercise 11- One- word

1. Which protocol manages encryption in Bluetooth communication?
2. What is the Bluetooth profile used for voice calls in vehicles?

Exercise 12- Small Answers

1. Explain the role of the Bluetooth protocol stack.
2. What are the main advantages of Bluetooth compared to Wi-Fi?

Exercise 13- Long Answers

1. Describe the applications and limitations of Bluetooth technology.
2. Compare Bluetooth with Wi-Fi in terms of power consumption, range, and speed.

Exercise 14- Previous Years Unsolved Questions

1. Explain how mobile computing influences business decision-making processes with real-time data. (Anna University, June 2022, MCA)
2. What are Progressive Web Apps (PWAs), and how do they fit into the mobile computing ecosystem? (IGNOU, December 2021, MCA)
3. How do mobile computing systems manage security for online banking applications? (Mumbai University, December 2023, MCA)
4. Describe the impact of mobile computing on remote work and distributed teams. (Anna University, July 2022, MCA)
5. What is hybrid mobile applications, and how do they differ from native and web apps? (IGNOU, December 2021, MCA)

6. How does edge computing enhance the performance of mobile computing devices? (Anna University, June 2022, MCA)
7. Discuss the role of mobile virtual private networks (VPNs) in ensuring secure mobile connectivity. (Mumbai University, December 2023, MCA)
8. What are the key challenges faced by developers when building cross-platform mobile apps? (Anna University, July 2022, MCA)
9. How does mobile computing impact cyber security? Provide examples of potential risks. (IGNOU, December 2021, MCA)
10. What is mobile middleware, and how does it support mobile computing systems? (Anna University, June 2022, MCA)
11. Explain the significance of API integration in mobile app development. (Mumbai University, December 2023, MCA)
12. How do mobile devices handle offline data access and synchronization? (IGNOU, December 2021, MCA)

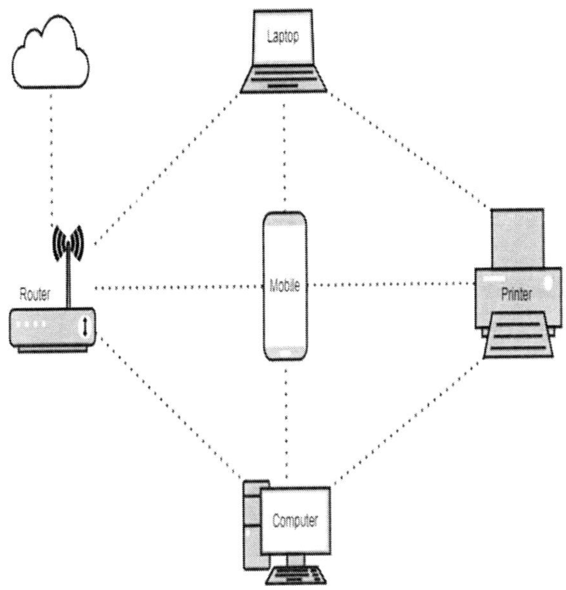

Answers

Exercise 1- 1. b) HFP. 2. c) NFC
Exercise 2- 1. True. 2. False
Exercise 3- 1. NFC. 2. protocol
Exercise 4- 1. low-power. 2. voice calls
Exercise 5- 1. Bluetooth is suitable for low-power tasks. 2. The protocol stack ensures secure communication.
Exercise 6. 1. d) Wi-Fi. 2. c) PAN
Exercise 7- 1. HFP. 2. BLUETOOTH
Exercise 8- 1. C. 2. B. 3. A. 4. d
Exercise 9- 1. c) Assertion is true, but the reason is false.
2. a) Both assertion and reason are true, and the reason is the correct explanation.
Exercise 10-

M	**H**	**F**	**P**	P	H	F	G	Q	T
I	N	C	N	R	A	S	D	I	A
H	**L**	P	C	F	R	H	L	P	X
T	**M**	Q	R	T	K	N	Y	I	W
I	**P**	W	A	N	B	N	M	F	V
P	L	A	N	Q	N	G	T	I	D
L	B	L	E	C	U	U	V	S	A
E	N	C	F	K	S	N	X	I	T
X	G	Y	T	J	E	S	W	O	A
S	O	X	S	V	R	E	S	N	S

Exercise 11- 1. LMP. 2. HFP

Test Paper
Chapter-7
Bluetooth and Short-Range Wireless Technologies

Time Duration: 30 Minutes **Maximum Marks: 25**

General Instructions:

1. The question paper consists of 12 questions and is divided into four sections, A, B, C and D.
2. All questions are compulsory.
3. Section A comprises MCQs, fill in the blanks and True or False carrying one marks each.
4. Section B comprises VSAQs (very short answers questions) carrying two marks each.
5. Section C comprises SAQs (short questions) carrying four marks each.
6. Section D comprises long questions carrying five marks each.

SECTION-A

Q1. Multiple choice questions: **(1*2=2)**

1. What is the Bluetooth profile used for voice calls in vehicles?

a) A2DP
b) HFP
c) NFC
d) LMP

2. Which technology is typically used for contactless transactions?

a) PAN
b) NFC
c) LMP
d) Bluetooth Protocol Stack

Q2. Fill in the blanks: **(1*2=2)**

1. Bluetooth communication uses the _____ GHz band for short-range wireless connectivity.
2. The _____ protocol layer manages encryption and secure communication in Bluetooth.

Q3. True or False: **(1*2=2)**

1. Bluetooth is better suited for high-speed data transfer than Wi-Fi.
2. LMP is a Bluetooth protocol layer that handles secure communication.

SECTION-B

Q4. Very Short answers type questions-I **(2*3=6)**

1. What is the purpose of the Bluetooth protocol stack?
2. Define a Personal Area Network (PAN) and give one example of its use.
3. List two limitations of Bluetooth technology.

SECTION-C

Q5. Short answers type questions-II **(4*2=8)**

1. Compare the advantages and limitations of Bluetooth technology.
2. Explain the difference between Bluetooth and Wi-Fi in terms of power consumption and speed.

SECTION-D

Q6. Long answers type questions **(5*1=5)**

1. Describe the various profiles and applications of Bluetooth technology, and explain how Bluetooth supports interoperability in IoT ecosystems.

Chapter 8 - Wireless Application Protocol (WAP)

In this chapter you will learn about:
- Introduction to Wireless Application Protocol
- WAP Architecture and Protocol Stack
- Components of WAP
- WAP Applications in Mobile Computing
- Challenges and Future of WAP

Wireless Application Protocol (WAP) is a standard that enables **mobile devices** such as smartphones and feature phones to access the Internet and online services over **wireless networks**. WAP bridges the gap between mobile networks and the Internet by converting web content into formats suitable for small screens with limited bandwidth. During the late 1990s and early 2000s, WAP played a crucial role in **mobile communication**, allowing users to browse websites, send emails, and access services like news and banking over slower mobile networks such as **2G**.

8.1 Introduction to Wireless Application Protocol (WAP)

WAP is a communication protocol that helps mobile devices connect to the web by providing a **unified standard** for wireless communication. It was developed to overcome the challenges of slow mobile networks, limited bandwidth, and restricted device capabilities. WAP ensures mobile users can access internet content and services with minimal data usage. The lightweight protocol focuses on **text-based communication and compressed data** to make mobile internet viable even on basic phones.

8.2 WAP Architecture and Protocol Stack

WAP uses a **layered protocol stack**, similar to other communication standards, to ensure smooth communication between devices and servers. Here are the key layers:

1. Application Layer (WAE - Wireless Application Environment):
- o Provides mobile-friendly services like web browsing and messaging.
- o Uses a markup language called WML (Wireless Markup Language) to format small-screen content.

2. Session Layer (WSP - Wireless Session Protocol):
- o Establishes and manages communication sessions between devices.
- o Similar to HTTP but optimised for mobile networks.

3. Transaction Layer (WTP - Wireless Transaction Protocol):
- o Ensures reliable data transmission, supporting confirmation messages and error checking.

4. Security Layer (WTLS - Wireless Transport Layer Security):
- o Provides encryption and authentication to protect data over wireless networks.

5. Transport Layer (WDP - Wireless Datagram Protocol):
- o Manages data transmission over various wireless networks like GSM and CDMA.

8.3 Components of WAP

WAP relies on several key components for its functionality:

- **Mobile Device (Client):** A phone or tablet with a WAP browser for accessing online content.
- **WAP Gateway:** This device acts as a bridge between the mobile network and the Internet, converting HTTP content into WAP-friendly formats.
- **WAP Server:** Hosts WML-based content specifically designed for mobile users.
- **Mobile Network:** A communication channel like GSM, CDMA, or GPRS that provides internet access to the mobile device.

8.4 WAP Applications in Mobile Computing

WAP was widely used in the early stages of mobile internet to provide **essential services**. Some of its common applications include:

1. Mobile Banking: Allowed users to check account balances and transfer funds.
2. Email Access: Enabled users to send and receive emails on feature phones.
3. News and Weather Updates: Provided real-time news feeds and weather forecasts.
4. Ringtones and Wallpapers: Users can download ringtones, wallpapers, and mobile content via WAP.
5. E-commerce: Facilitated mobile shopping with limited functionality on early websites.

8.5 Challenges and Future of WAP

Despite its early success, WAP faced several challenges:

1. **Limited User Experience:** The text-based interface and WML format could not match the visual appeal of modern web pages.
2. **Slow Speeds:** WAP was limited by the data transfer rates of 2G and early 3G networks.
3. **Complex Setup:** Users needed to configure WAP settings manually, which was inconvenient.
4. **Security Concerns:** While WTLS offered encryption, it wasn't as robust as modern HTTPS.
5. **Obsolescence:** With the rise of faster networks like 4G and 5G, and HTML5-based websites, WAP became outdated.

Future:
Though WAP is no longer widely used, its development marked the beginning of **mobile-friendly web technologies**. Today, technologies like **responsive web design** and **mobile applications** carry forward its legacy by offering seamless mobile internet experiences.

8.6 Glossary

- **WML (Wireless Markup Language):** A markup language used in WAP for displaying content on mobile screens.
- **WTLS (Wireless Transport Layer Security):** Security protocol used in WAP to encrypt data.
- **WAP Gateway:** A server that converts internet data into WAP-compatible formats.
- **GPRS (General Packet Radio Service):** A mobile data service used in early 2G and 3G networks.
- **Session**: A temporary connection between devices for data exchange.

8.7 Summary

- WAP is a communication protocol that allows mobile devices to access online content over wireless networks.
- The WAP protocol stack has layers, including WAE (Application), WSP (Session), WTP (Transaction), WTLS (Security), and WDP (Transport).
- Key components of WAP include the mobile device, WAP gateway, WAP server, and the mobile network.
- WAP applications included mobile banking, email access, news updates, and ringtones.
- WAP faced challenges like slow speeds, limited user experience, and complex setup, leading to its decline with the advent of 4G and modern web technologies.
- Though obsolete, WAP played a critical role in mobile internet history and paved the way for mobile-friendly technologies today.

8.8 Previous Year Solved Question

Question: What are the key layers of the WAP protocol stack? Explain the role of each layer. (Anna University, July 2022, MCA)
Answer: The WAP protocol stack consists of the following layers:

1. WAE (Wireless Application Environment): Provides mobile-friendly services and uses WML for content display.
2. WSP (Wireless Session Protocol): Manages sessions between devices, optimising mobile communication.
3. WTP (Wireless Transaction Protocol): Ensures reliable data transmission through confirmations and error checks.
4. WTLS (Wireless Transport Layer Security): Protects data with encryption and authentication.
5. WDP (Wireless Datagram Protocol): Handles data transport over various mobile networks like GPRS.

Exercises

Exercise 1 – Multiple Choice Questions

1. Which markup language was used in WAP for mobile content display?

   a) WML
   b) HTML
   c) XML
   d) CSS

2. What protocol was used to encrypt data in WAP communications?

   a) SSL
   b) WTLS
   c) TLS
   d) HTTPS

Exercise 2 – True/False

1. WML was used to display content on mobile screens through WAP.
2. WAP technology became more popular after the arrival of 4G networks.

Exercise 3 – Fill in the blanks

1. ______ is the security protocol used in WAP to encrypt data.
2. A ______ converts internet data into WAP-compatible formats.

Exercise 4- Fill in the blanks with two options

1. ______ (GPRS/HTTPS) was used for mobile data services in early 2G and 3G networks.
2. A ______ (session/transaction) is a temporary connection between devices for data exchange.

Exercise 5- Rearrange the sentence

1. Protocol / online / communication / content / mobile / A / access / WAP / wireless / over / for / networks.
2. Mobile / banking / included / WAP / applications / access / and / email.

Exercise 6- Choose the Odd One Out

1. a) GPRS
   b) WTLS
   c) WML
   d) 4G
2. a) Session
   b) Transaction
   c) WDP
   d) WAP Gateway

Exercise 7- Jumble words

1. LWM (Hint: Used to display mobile content in WAP)
2. SLSWT (Hint: Security protocol used in WAP)

Exercise 8- Match case

1. WML
2. WTLS
3. WAP Gateway
4. GPRS

a) Converts internet data into WAP formats
b) Mobile data service for 2G/3G networks

c) Security protocol for data encryption
d) Markup language for mobile screens

Exercise 9- Assertion – Reason

1. **Assertion:** WAP technology laid the foundation for mobile-friendly web technologies.
Reason: WAP was widely used in 4G networks.
a) Both assertion and reason are true, and the reason is the correct explanation.
b) Both assertion and reason are true, but the reason is not the correct explanation.
c) Assertion is true, but the reason is false.
d) Both assertion and reason are false.

2. **Assertion:** WTLS is used to encrypt data in WAP communication.
Reason: WTLS belongs to the WAP security layer in the protocol stack.
a) Both assertion and reason are true, and the reason is the correct explanation.
b) Both assertion and reason are true, but the reason is not the correct explanation.
c) Assertion is true, but the reason is false.
d) Both assertion and reason are false.

Exercise 10- Read the questions below and find the appropriate word in the provided grid.

1. Find the server that converts internet data into WAP-compatible formats.
2. Identify the security protocol used in WAP communications.

W	A	P	G	A	T	E	W	A	Y
W	M	L	N	E	F	S	I	M	A
L	P	G	R	S	A	T	L	K	X
T	O	Q	G	T	P	W	Y	I	W
I	I	W	P	N	B	N	M	F	V
P	L	A	R	Q	N	G	T	I	D
L	B	L	S	C	U	U	V	S	A
E	N	C	F	K	S	N	X	I	T
X	G	Y	T	J	E	S	W	O	A
S	O	X	S	V	R	E	S	N	S

Exercise 11- One- word

1. What protocol converts internet data into WAP-compatible formats?
2. What mobile data service was used in early 2G and 3G networks?

Exercise 12- Small Answers

1. What challenges led to the decline of WAP?
2. How did WAP pave the way for modern mobile technologies?

Exercise 13- Long Answers

1. Describe the WAP protocol stack and its components.
2. Explain the evolution of WAP and its importance in mobile internet history.

Exercise 14- Previous Years Unsolved Questions

1. Discuss the role of responsive design in enhancing mobile computing experiences. (Anna University, July 2022, MCA)
2. What are mobile payment gateways, and how do they ensure secure transactions? (Anna University, June 2022, MCA)
3. Explain the differences between Wi-Fi, LTE, and 5G technologies in mobile computing. (IGNOU, December 2021, MCA)
4. How do wearable devices like smart watches integrate with mobile computing systems? (Mumbai University, December 2023, MCA)

5. What is the role of machine learning in mobile computing applications? Provide examples. (Anna University, July 2022, MCA)
6. Discuss the impact of mobile computing on supply chain management. (Anna University, June 2022, MCA)
7. Explain the concept of geo fencing and its applications in mobile computing. (IGNOU, December 2021, MCA)
8. How does augmented reality (AR) work on mobile devices? Provide examples. (Mumbai University, December 2023, MCA)
9. What are mobile enterprise applications, and how do they benefit organizations? (Anna University, July 2022, MCA)

Answers

Exercise 1- 1. a) WML. 2. b) WTLS
Exercise 2- 1. True. 2. False
Exercise 3- 1. WTLS. 2. WAP Gateway
Exercise 4- 1. GPRS. 2. Session
Exercise 5- 1. WAP is a communication protocol for accessing online content over wireless networks.
2. WAP applications included mobile banking and email access.
Exercise 6- 1. d) 4G. 2. b) Session
Exercise 7- 1. WML. 2. WTLS
Exercise 8- 1. D. 2. C. 3. A. 4. b
Exercise 9- 1. c) Assertion is true, but the reason is false.
2. a) Both assertion and reason are true, and the reason is the correct explanation.
Exercise 10-

W	**A**	**P**	**G**	**A**	**T**	**E**	**W**	**A**	**Y**
W	M	L	N	E	F	S	I	M	A
L	P	G	R	S	A	T	L	K	X
T	O	Q	**G**	T	P	W	Y	I	W
I	I	W	**P**	N	B	N	M	F	V
P	L	A	**R**	Q	N	G	T	I	D
L	B	L	**S**	C	U	U	V	S	A
E	N	C	F	K	S	N	X	I	T
X	G	Y	T	J	E	S	W	O	A
S	O	X	S	V	R	E	S	N	S

Exercise 11- 1. WAP Gateway. 2. GPRS

Test Paper

Chapter-8
Wireless Application Protocol (WAP)

Time Duration: 30 Minutes **Maximum Marks: 25**

General Instructions:

1. The question paper consists of 12 questions and is divided into four sections, A, B, C and D.
2. All questions are compulsory.
3. Section A comprises MCQs, fill in the blanks and True or False carrying one marks each.
4. Section B comprises VSAQs (very short answers questions) carrying two marks each.
5. Section C comprises SAQs (short questions) carrying four marks each.
6. Section D comprises long questions carrying five marks each.

SECTION-A

Q1. Multiple choice questions: **(1*2=2)**

1. Which protocol is used in WAP to encrypt data for secure communication?

a) GPRS
b) WTLS
c) WML
d) WAP Gateway

2. What is the role of the WAP Gateway in mobile communication?

a) Encrypt data
b) Manage sessions
c) Convert internet data into WAP-compatible formats
d) Provide ringtones

Q2. Fill in the blanks: **(1*2=2)**

1. WML is a ______ used to display content on mobile screens through WAP.
2. A ______ in WAP is a temporary connection established between devices for data exchange.

Q3. True or False: **(1*2=2)**

1. WAP allows mobile devices to access online content over wireless networks.
2. WAP replaced 4G technology as the primary mobile communication protocol.

SECTION-B

Q4. Very Short answers type questions-I **(2*3=6)**

1. What are the key components of the WAP protocol?
2. Mention two applications of WAP.
3. Why did WAP decline with the advent of modern web technologies?

SECTION-C

Q5. Short answers type questions-II **(4*2=8)**

1. Explain the WAP protocol stack and its layers.
2. Describe the role of GPRS in early mobile networks.

SECTION-D

Q6. Long answers type questions **(5*1=5)**

1. Discuss the importance of WAP in mobile internet history and how it paved the way for modern mobile-friendly technologies.

Chapter 9 - Mobile IP and Mobility Management

In this chapter you will learn about:

- Introduction to Mobile IP
- What a Mobile IP Works
- Mobility Management in Mobile Networks
- Challenges in Mobile IP Implementation
- Solutions and Protocols for Mobile IP

Mobile IP (Internet Protocol) is a communication protocol that enables mobile devices to maintain network connectivity even as they move across different networks. It allows devices to seamlessly switch between networks—from a **home network** to a **foreign one**—without losing their IP address or active sessions. Developed by the Internet Engineering Task Force (IETF), Mobile IP is essential for **mobility management** in mobile networks, ensuring that users can stay connected while travelling across different geographic regions or networks. It plays a critical role in supporting **mobile computing**, particularly for smartphones, tablets, and IoT devices.

9.1 Introduction to Mobile IP

Mobile IP solves a fundamental problem in traditional IP networks: **maintaining continuous internet connectivity** as devices move from one network to another. In standard IP communication, a device's IP address changes when it connects to a new network, leading to disruptions. Mobile IP ensures that a mobile device can **retain its original IP address** while roaming between networks, maintaining active sessions and ensuring smooth communication.

9.2 How Mobile IP Works

The operation of Mobile IP involves several key components and processes:

1. **Home Agent (HA):**
   a. A router in the home network that keeps track of the mobile device's current location.
   b. It forwards data to the device's current network when it is away from the home network.
2. **Foreign Agent (FA):**
   a. A router in the foreign network that assigns a temporary Care-of Address (CoA) to the mobile device.
   b. It helps route data packets to the mobile device while connected to the foreign network.
3. **Correspondent Node (CN):** A device or server communicating with the mobile device, unaware of its movements.
4. **Process Flow:**
   a. When a mobile device connects to a new (foreign) network, it registers with the Foreign Agent, which assigns a Care-of Address (CoA).
   b. The Foreign Agent informs the Home Agent of the new address.
   c. The Home Agent intercepts data packets from the Correspondent Node and tunnels them to the CoA.
   d. The Foreign Agent forwards the packets to the mobile device, ensuring uninterrupted communication.

9.3 Mobility Management in Mobile Networks

Mobility management ensures that mobile devices can **maintain seamless communication** between networks. It involves two key aspects:

1. **Handover Management:**
   a. Ensures a smooth transition when a mobile device switches from one network to another (e.g., Wi-Fi to mobile data).
   b. Reduces delays and avoids dropped calls or interrupted sessions.
2. **Location Management:**
   a. Tracks the mobile device's location and updates the network to ensure data is routed correctly.
   b. This process relies on the Home Agent and Foreign Agent to manage IP addresses effectively.

9.4 Challenges in Mobile IP Implementation

Implementing Mobile IP presents several challenges:

a. **Latency Issues:** Switching between networks can introduce delays, affecting real-time applications like voice and video calls.
b. **Security Risks:** Mobile IP can be vulnerable to attacks, such as session hijacking and spoofing.
c. **Scalability Issues:** Managing a large number of mobile devices becomes complex for service providers.
d. **Tunneling Overhead:** The process of tunnelling data through Home Agents adds extra data load, reducing network efficiency.

9.5 Solutions and Protocols for Mobile IP

Several solutions and protocols have been developed to address the challenges of Mobile IP:

a. **Mobile IPv6:** An improved version of Mobile IP that supports IPv6 networks with enhanced security and mobility features.

b. **Fast Handover Protocols:** Reduces latency during network switching by preparing the new network before the handover occurs.

c. **Authentication Protocols:** Encryption and authentication mechanisms are used to secure data transmission and prevent unauthorised access.

d. **Hierarchical Mobile IP (HMIP):** Introduces multiple layers of management to improve scalability and efficiency.

9.6 Glossary

1. **Home Agent (HA):** A router in the home network that manages the mobile device's location.
2. **Foreign Agent (FA):** A router in the foreign network that assigns a temporary Care-of Address to the device.
3. **Care-of Address (CoA):** A temporary IP address assigned to a device when it connects to a foreign network.
4. **Correspondent Node (CN):** The device or server communicating with the mobile device.
5. **Tunneling:** Encapsulating data packets to transmit them across networks.

9.7 Summary

- Mobile IP allows devices to maintain their original IP address while switching between networks, ensuring seamless communication.
- How a Mobile IP Works: It involves Home Agents (HA), foreign agents (FA), and Correspondent Nodes (CN) to manage data transfer and device location.
- Mobility Management: Consists of handover and location management to ensure uninterrupted communication.
- Challenges: Mobile IP faces latency, security risks, scalability concerns, and tunnelling overhead.
- Solutions: Protocols like Mobile IPv6, Fast Handover, and Hierarchical Mobile IP (HMIP) address these challenges and improve performance.

9.8 Previous Year Solved Question

Question: What are the key components of Mobile IP, and how do they ensure uninterrupted communication? (Mumbai University, December 2023, MCA)

Answer: Mobile IP relies on three main components:

1. **Home Agent (HA):**
    a. Manages the mobile device's location in its home network.
    b. Forwards data to the device's current network when it is away from the home network.
2. **Foreign Agent (FA):**
    a. Assigns a Care-of Address (CoA) to the device when it connects to a foreign network.
    b. Ensures data is routed correctly to the mobile device.
3. **Correspondent Node (CN):**
    a. A device or server communicating with the mobile device.
    b. Sends data to the Home Agent, unaware of the device's network movement.

These components work together to ensure that data packets reach the mobile device even as it switches between networks, providing a seamless communication experience.

Exercises

Exercise 1 – Multiple Choice Questions

1. What is the role of the Foreign Agent (FA) in Mobile IP?

a) Manages the original IP address of the mobile device
b) Assigns a temporary Care-of Address (CoA)
c) Encapsulates data packets for tunneling
d) Acts as a Correspondent Node

2. What process encapsulates data packets for transmission across networks in Mobile IP?

a) Routing
b) Tunneling
c) Forwarding
d) Switching

Exercise 2 – True/False

1. The Home Agent (HA) manages the original IP address of the mobile device.
2. Mobile IP ensures seamless communication by frequently changing the original IP address of the device.

Exercise 3 – Fill in the blanks

1. A _____ is a device or server communicating with the mobile device in Mobile IP.
2. The process of encapsulating data packets to transmit them across networks is called _____.

Exercise 4- Fill in the blanks with two options

1. A temporary IP address assigned in a foreign network is called a _____ (Care-of Address/Home Agent).
2. _____ (Tunneling/Forwarding) encapsulates data packets for transmission across networks.

Exercise 5- Rearrange the sentence

1. Mobile / while / IP / address / devices / maintain / allows / switching / networks / between / their / original.
2. Consists / management / mobility / uninterrupted / communication / ensuring / of / location / handover / and.

Exercise 6- Choose the Odd One Out

1. a) Care-of Address (CoA)
b) Home Agent (HA)
c) Correspondent Node (CN)
d) IPv6
2. a) Handover Management
b) Location Management
c) Routing Management
d) Mobility Management

Exercise 7- Jumble words

1. GNILEUNNT (Hint: Encapsulation process in Mobile IP)
2. COFA (Hint: Temporary IP address assigned in a foreign network)

Exercise 8- Match case

1. Home Agent (HA)
2. Foreign Agent (FA)
3. Care-of Address (CoA)
4. Tunneling

a) Encapsulates data packets for transmission
b) Router that assigns a temporary IP address
c) Temporary IP address assigned in a foreign network
d) Manages the mobile device's original IP address

Exercise 9- Assertion – Reason

1. **Assertion:** Tunneling encapsulates data packets to transmit them across networks.
Reason: Tunneling reduces network latency in Mobile IP.
a) Both assertion and reason are true, and the reason is the correct explanation.
b) Both assertion and reason are true, but the reason is not the correct explanation.
c) Assertion is true, but the reason is false.
d) Both assertion and reason are false.

2. **Assertion:** Foreign Agents assign Care-of Addresses to devices in foreign networks.
Reason: Foreign Agents handle mobility management to ensure uninterrupted communication.
a) Both assertion and reason are true, and the reason is the correct explanation.
b) Both assertion and reason are true, but the reason is not the correct explanation.
c) Assertion is true, but the reason is false.
d) Both assertion and reason are false.

Exercise 10- Read the questions below and find the appropriate word in the provided grid.

1. Identify the router that assigns a temporary Care-of Address to a device.
2. Find the process used to encapsulate data packets for transmission.

C	O	A	P	H	T	U	N	N	L
A	G	E	N	T	F	S	I	I	A
L	C	R	S	G	A	T	N	U	X
T	O	Q	R	O	P	W	Y	N	W
I	I	W	A	F	B	N	M	N	V
P	L	A	N	Q	N	G	T	E	D
L	B	L	E	C	U	U	V	L	A
E	N	C	F	K	S	N	X	I	T
X	G	Y	T	J	E	S	W	N	A
S	O	X	S	V	R	E	S	G	S

Exercise 11- One- word

1. Which router assigns a temporary IP address to a device in a foreign network?
2. What process is used to encapsulate data packets for transmission across networks?

Exercise 12- Small Answers

1. What challenges does Mobile IP face?
2. How do protocols like Mobile IPv6 improve Mobile IP performance?

Exercise 13- Long Answers

1. Explain how Mobile IP works, detailing the role of Home Agents, Foreign Agents, and Correspondent Nodes.
2. Describe the concept of mobility management in Mobile IP and the solutions to its challenges.

Exercise 14- Previous Years Unsolved Questions

1. Discuss the concept of responsive web design and its importance in mobile computing. (Anna University, June 2022, MCA)
2. Explain the significance of caching in mobile computing applications. (IGNOU, December 2021, MCA)
3. What are the advantages and disadvantages of biometric authentication in mobile computing? (Mumbai University, December 2023, MCA)
4. How does the Internet of Things (IoT) leverage mobile computing for real-time data exchange? (Anna University, July 2022, MCA)
5. What is the impact of mobile computing on customer relationship management (CRM)? (Anna University, June 2022, MCA)

6. Explain the difference between mobile analytics and web analytics. (IGNOU, December 2021, MCA)
7. How do push notifications impact user engagement in mobile applications? (Mumbai University, December 2023, MCA)
8. Discuss the concept of mobile commerce and its influence on consumer behavior. (Anna University, July 2022, MCA)
9. What are the primary differences between Bluetooth Low Energy (BLE) and traditional Bluetooth in mobile computing? (Anna University, June 2022, MCA)
10. Explain the role of cloud computing in mobile app development. (IGNOU, December 2021, MCA)
11. How do content delivery networks (CDNs) optimize mobile computing performance? (Mumbai University, December 2023, MCA)
12. What is the impact of mobile computing on personal data privacy? (Anna University, July 2022, MCA)
13. Describe the concept of app monetization in mobile computing. Provide examples. (Anna University, June 2022, MCA)
14. How do mobile computing technologies support telemedicine services? (IGNOU, December 2021, MCA)
15. Discuss the benefits and challenges of integrating artificial intelligence (AI) with mobile applications. (Mumbai University, December 2023, MCA)

Answers

Exercise 1- 1. b) Assigns a temporary Care-of Address (CoA). 2. b) Tunnelling
Exercise 2- 1. True. 2. False
Exercise 3- 1. Correspondent Node (CN). 2. Tunnelling
Exercise 4- 1. Care-of Address. 2. Tunnelling
Exercise 5- 1. Mobile IP allows devices to maintain their original IP address while switching between networks.
2. Mobility management consists of handover and location management.
Exercise 6 1. d) IPv6. 2. c) Routing Management
Exercise 7- 1. TUNNELING. 2. COFA
Exercise 8- 1. D. 2. B. 3. C. 4. a
Exercise 9- 1. c) Assertion is true, but the reason is false.
2. b) Both assertion and reason are true, but the reason is not the correct explanation.
Exercise 10-

C	O	A	P	H	T	U	N	N	L
A	**G**	**E**	**N**	**T**	F	S	I	**T**	A
L	C	R	S	G	A	T	N	**U**	X
T	O	Q	R	O	P	W	Y	**N**	W
I	I	W	A	F	B	N	M	**N**	V
P	L	A	N	Q	N	G	T	**E**	D
L	B	L	E	C	U	U	V	**L**	A
E	N	C	F	K	S	N	X	**I**	T
X	G	Y	T	J	E	S	W	**N**	A
S	O	X	S	V	R	E	S	**G**	S

Exercise 11- 1. Foreign Agent (FA). 2. Tunnelling

Test Paper
Chapter-9
Mobile IP and Mobility Management

Time Duration: 30 Minutes **Maximum Marks: 25**

General Instructions:

1. The question paper consists of 12 questions and is divided into four sections, A, B, C and D.
2. All questions are compulsory.
3. Section A comprises MCQs, fill in the blanks and True or False carrying one marks each.
4. Section B comprises VSAQs (very short answers questions) carrying two marks each.
5. Section C comprises SAQs (short questions) carrying four marks each.
6. Section D comprises long questions carrying five marks each.

SECTION-A

Q1. Multiple choice questions: **(1*2=2)**

1. Which router in the home network manages the location of the mobile device?

a) Foreign Agent (FA)
b) Home Agent (HA)
c) Correspondent Node (CN)
d) Care-of Address (CoA)

2. What is the process of encapsulating data packets for transmission across networks called?

a) Routing
b) Forwarding
c) Tunneling
d) Handover

Q2. Fill in the blanks: **(1*2=2)**

1. A _____ is assigned to a mobile device as a temporary IP address when it connects to a foreign network.
2. The _____ node is the device or server that communicates with the mobile device.

Q3. True or False: **(1*2=2)**

1. Mobile IP allows devices to maintain their original IP address while switching between networks.
2. Tunneling reduces security risks in Mobile IP networks.

SECTION-B

Q4. Very Short answers type questions-I **(2*3=6)**

1. What is the role of the Home Agent (HA) in Mobile IP?
2. Define tunneling in the context of Mobile IP.
3. Name two challenges Mobile IP faces.

SECTION-C

Q5. Short answers type questions-II **(4*2=8)**

1. Explain how Foreign Agents (FA) and Home Agents (HA) work together to manage mobile devices in Mobile IP.
2. How do Mobile IPv6 and Fast Handover protocols address the challenges of Mobile IP?

SECTION-D

Q6. Long answers type questions **(5*1=5)**

1. Discuss the significance of Mobile IP in ensuring seamless communication and explain how mobility management plays a role in uninterrupted communication.

Chapter 10 - Emerging Trends in Mobile Computing

In this chapter you will learn about:
- Evolution of Mobile Networks: 1G to 5G
- Internet of Things (IoT) in Mobile Computing
- Edge Computing and Mobile Networks
- Future Trends in Mobile CommunicationAI and Machine Learning in Mobile Computing

The evolution of mobile networks and computing has transformed how we communicate, work, and live. From **1G networks** that only supported voice calls to **5G** and **beyond**, mobile networks have become the backbone of digital communication. The rise of the **Internet of Things (IoT)** has expanded the role of mobile networks, enabling smart devices to communicate seamlessly.

10.1 Evolution of Mobile Networks: 1G to 5G and Beyond

Mobile networks have evolved across multiple generations, each introducing new features and capabilities:

- **1G (First Generation):**
  a. Introduced in the 1980s with analog technology supporting voice calls only.
  b. Limited capacity, low sound quality, and no data transmission.
- **2G (Second Generation):**
  a. Launched in the 1990s with digital technology.
  b. Enabled text messaging (SMS) and multimedia messaging (MMS).
- **3G (Third Generation):**
  a. Introduced mobile internet with data speeds suitable for web browsing and video calling.
  b. Paved the way for smartphones and mobile applications.
- **4G (Fourth Generation):**
  a. Focused on high-speed internet, enabling HD video streaming, online gaming, and IoT devices.
  b. Improved mobile network stability and latency.
- **5G (Fifth Generation):**
  a. Offers ultra-fast data speeds, low latency, and higher network capacity.
  b. Powers innovations like autonomous vehicles, IoT ecosystems, and smart cities.
- **Beyond 5G:** Research is underway for 6G, focusing on even faster communication, AI integration, and quantum networks.

10.2 Internet of Things (IoT) in Mobile Computing

The **Internet of Things (IoT)** is a network of interconnected devices that collect and exchange data. In mobile computing, IoT has transformed various industries by enabling smart devices to communicate seamlessly:

Examples of IoT Devices:

a. Smart Home Devices: Thermostats, security cameras, and voice assistants.
b. Wearable's: Fitness trackers, smartwatches, and healthcare monitors.
c. Connected Vehicles: Autonomous cars with real-time communication systems.

IoT devices rely on mobile networks for continuous connectivity, ensuring real-time data transmission and remote monitoring capabilities.

10.3 Edge Computing and Mobile Networks

Edge computing refers to processing data closer to where it is generated, reducing the need to send data to distant cloud servers. This approach improves performance and lowers latency.

- **Role in Mobile Networks:**
  a. Edge computing allows mobile devices to perform complex tasks with minimal delay by offloading some processing to nearby nodes.
  b. It supports time-sensitive applications like autonomous vehicles and industrial IoT.
- **Examples of Edge Computing Applications:**
  a. Smart Traffic Systems: Process traffic data locally to optimise signal timings.
  b. Augmented Reality (AR): Edge nodes handle real-time processing for smooth AR experiences.

10.4 Future Trends in Mobile Communication

Several trends are shaping the future of mobile communication:

a. 6G Networks: Expected to offer speeds 100 times faster than 5G with integrated AI support.
b. Satellite-Based Internet: Projects like Star Link aim to provide global internet coverage using satellite networks.

c. Smart Cities and IoT Ecosystems: Mobile networks will be crucial in connecting devices across smart cities, enabling better resource management.

d. Holographic Communication: Holograms for virtual meetings are expected to become more mainstream with advancements in mobile networks.

10.5 AI and Machine Learning in Mobile Computing

AI and machine learning are transforming mobile computing by enabling smarter and more efficient services:

a. Personalized Experiences: Virtual assistants like Google Assistant and Siri use AI to offer personalized recommendations.

b. Predictive Maintenance: Mobile networks equipped with AI can detect and address faults before they cause disruptions.

c. AI-Powered Apps: Apps use machine learning algorithms for face recognition, voice recognition, and real-time translations.

d. Network Optimization: AI helps mobile operators manage network traffic efficiently, improving the user experience.

10.6 Glossary

1. **1G-5G:** Different generations of mobile networks with increasing data speeds and capabilities.
2. **IoT (Internet of Things):** A network of devices that communicate with each other over the Internet.
3. **Edge Computing:** Processing data close to where it is generated to reduce latency.
4. **6G Networks:** The next generation of mobile networks is expected to succeed 5G.
5. **Machine Learning:** A subset of AI that enables systems to learn and improve from data without being explicitly programmed.

10.7 Summary

- **Evolution of Mobile Networks:** From 1G's analog voice calls to 5G's ultra-fast internet, mobile networks have significantly improved communication and data transmission.
- **IoT in Mobile Computing:** IoT devices rely on mobile networks for continuous connectivity, enabling smart homes, connected vehicles, and wearable devices.
- **Edge Computing:** Reduces latency by processing data close to the source, supporting time-sensitive applications like AR and smart traffic systems.
- **Future Trends:** Developments such as 6G, satellite-based internet, and holographic communication will shape the future of mobile networks.
- **AI in Mobile Computing:** AI powers predictive maintenance, network optimization, and personalized services, improving the overall mobile computing experience.

10.8 Previous Year Solved Question

Question: Describe the evolution of mobile networks from 1G to 5G. Highlight the key features and advancements in each generation. (IGNOU, December 2021, MCA)

Answer:

1. **1G (First Generation):**
   a. Introduced analog technology for voice calls in the 1980s.
   b. Limited capacity and low call quality.
2. **2G (Second Generation):**
   a. Introduced digital technology, enabling SMS and MMS.
   b. Improved voice quality and capacity.
3. **3G (Third Generation):**
   a. Brought mobile internet and video calling.
   b. Paved the way for smart phones and apps.
4. **4G (Fourth Generation):**
   a. Focused on high-speed data transmission, enabling HD streaming and gaming.
   b. Improved network stability and introduced IoT support.
5. **5G (Fifth Generation):**
   a. Provides ultra-fast speeds, low latency, and high capacity.
   b. Supports technologies like autonomous vehicles and smart cities.

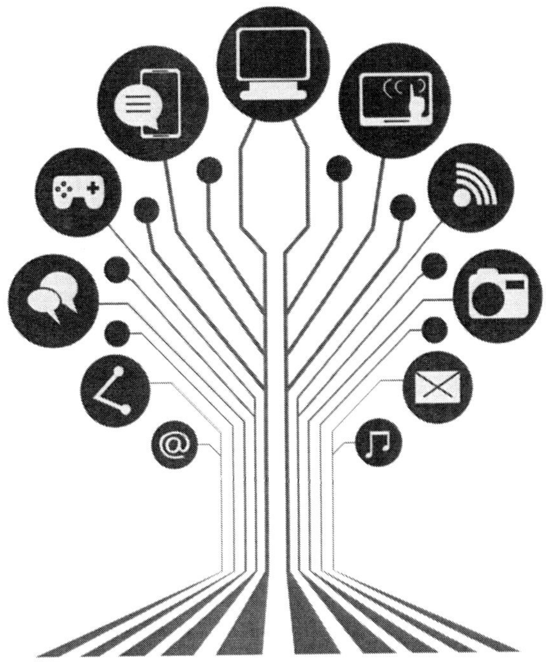

Exercises

Exercise 1 – Multiple Choice Questions

1. What is the primary benefit of edge computing in mobile networks?

a) Increases network bandwidth
b) Reduces latency
c) Enhances call quality
d) Decreases device power consumption

2. What is 6G expected to achieve?

a) Succeed 4G networks
b) Provide analog voice calls
c) Succeed 5G networks
d) Replace machine learning in mobile networks

Exercise 2 – True/False

1. IoT devices rely on mobile networks for continuous connectivity.
2. 1G network were known for high-speed internet access.

Exercise 3 – Fill in the blanks

1. _____ computing processes data close to its source to reduce latency.
2. _____ is the network of devices communicating over the internet.

Exercise 4- Fill in the blanks with two options

1. Mobile networks are evolving towards _____ (5G/6G), enabling new technologies like holographic communication.
2. _____ (Machine learning/IoT) allows systems to improve from data without explicit programming.

Exercise 5- Rearrange the sentence

1. Networks / improved / data / transmission / significantly / communication / Mobile / and / have.
2. Continuous / devices / rely / IoT / mobile / on / connectivity / networks / for.

Exercise 6- Choose the Odd One Out

1. a) 1G

b) 6G
c) 5G
d) IoT

2. a) Smart homes

b) Connected vehicles
c) Analog voice calls
d) Wearable devices

Exercise 7- Jumble words

1. GEED (Hint: Computing method that reduces latency)
2. IG6 (Hint: Future mobile network generation)

Exercise 8- Match case

1. IoT
2. 6G
3. Edge Computing
4. Machine Learning

a) Future mobile network succeeding 5G
b) Network of interconnected devices
c) Reduces latency by processing data near its source
d) Enables systems to learn from data

Exercise 9- Assertion – Reason

1. **Assertion:** Edge computing reduces latency in mobile networks.

Reason: Edge computing processes data at remote data centers.

a) Both assertion and reason are true, and the reason is the correct explanation.
b) Both assertion and reason are true, but the reason is not the correct explanation.
c) Assertion is true, but the reason is false.
d) Both assertion and reason are false.

2. **Assertion**: 6G networks will offer faster data speeds than 5G.

Reason: 6G networks will rely on IoT devices for network optimization.

a) Both assertion and reason are true, and the reason is the correct explanation.
b) Both assertion and reason are true, but the reason is not the correct explanation.
c) Assertion is true, but the reason is false.
d) Both assertion and reason are false.

Exercise 10- Read the questions below and find the appropriate word in the provided grid.

1. Identify the next generation of mobile networks expected to succeed 5G.
2. Find the computing method that reduces latency by processing data near its source.

6	G	E	D	G	M	I	T	N	X
M	L	G	N	A	F	P	L	I	A
I	O	T	R	S	A	T	N	F	X
L	P	E	D	G	E	P	T	K	T
T	I	W	A	F	B	N	M	F	V
P	L	A	N	Q	N	G	T	I	D
L	B	L	E	C	U	U	V	S	A
E	N	C	F	K	S	N	X	I	T
X	G	Y	T	J	E	S	W	O	A
S	O	X	S	V	R	E	S	N	S

Exercise 11- One- word

1. What is the network of devices communicating over the internet called?
2. Which future mobile network generation is expected to succeed 5G?

Exercise 12- Small Answers

1. How does edge computing support time-sensitive applications?
2. What role does machine learning play in mobile networks?

Exercise 13- Long Answers

1. Describe the evolution of mobile networks from 1G to 5G and the role of 6G in the future.
2. Explain the importance of IoT and edge computing in mobile computing.

Exercise 14- Previous Year Unsolved Questions

1. What is the different app distribution platforms used in mobile computing? (Anna University, July 2022, MCA)
2. How does encryption secure data transmission in mobile computing environments? (Anna University, June 2022, MCA)
3. Explain the concept of crowd sourcing through mobile platforms. (IGNOU, December 2021, MCA)
4. How do mobile computing solutions support inventory management systems? (Mumbai University, December 2023, MCA)
5. What is the role of voice assistants in mobile computing applications? Provide examples. (Anna University, July 2022, MCA)
6. Discuss the impact of mobile computing on the gaming industry. (Anna University, June 2022, MCA)
7. What is the role of Progressive Web Apps (PWAs) in mobile computing? (IGNOU, December 2021, MCA)

8. How do mobile computing technologies enhance user experience in smart homes? (Mumbai University, December 2023, MCA)

9. Explain how mobile devices manage energy consumption during heavy usage. (Anna University, July 2022, MCA)

10. What are the primary security concerns when using public Wi-Fi networks for mobile computing? (Anna University, June 2022, MCA)

11. Discuss the advantages and limitations of virtual mobile infrastructure (VMI). (IGNOU, December 2021, MCA)

12. How do mobile operating systems handle app permissions and user privacy? (Mumbai University, December 2023, MCA)

13. What are the challenges of implementing block chain technology in mobile computing? (Anna University, July 2022, MCA)

14. Explain how mobile computing influences modern marketing strategies, such as location-based advertising. (Anna University, June 2022, MCA)

Answers

Exercise 1- 1. b) Reduces latency. 2. c) Succeed 5G networks
Exercise 2- 1. True. 2. False
Exercise 3- 1. Edge. 2. IoT
Exercise 4- 1. 6G. 2. Machine learning
Exercise 5- 1. Mobile networks have significantly improved communication and data transmission.
2. IoT devices rely on mobile networks for continuous connectivity.
Exercise 6. 1. d) IoT. 2. c) Analog voice calls
Exercise 7- 1. EDGE. 2. 6G
Exercise 8- 1. B. 2. A. 3. C. 4. d
Exercise 9- 1. c) Assertion is true, but the reason is false.,
2. b) Both assertion and reason are true, but the reason is not the correct explanation.
Exercise 10-

6	**G**	E	D	G	M	I	T	N	X
M	L	G	N	A	F	P	L	I	A
I	O	T	R	S	A	T	N	E	X
L	P	**E**	**D**	**G**	**E**	P	T	K	T
T	I	W	A	F	B	N	M	F	V
P	L	A	N	Q	N	G	T	I	D
L	B	L	E	C	U	U	V	S	A
E	N	C	F	K	S	N	X	I	T
X	G	Y	T	J	E	S	W	O	A
S	O	X	S	V	R	E	S	N	S

Exercise 11- 1. IoT. 2. 6G

Test Paper

Chapter-10

Emerging Trends in Mobile Computing

Time Duration: 30 Minutes **Maximum Marks: 25**

General Instructions:

1. The question paper consists of 12 questions and is divided into four sections, A, B, C and D.
2. All questions are compulsory.
3. Section A comprises MCQs, fill in the blanks and True or False carrying one marks each.
4. Section B comprises VSAQs (very short answers questions) carrying two marks each.
5. Section C comprises SAQs (short questions) carrying four marks each.
6. Section D comprises long questions carrying five marks each.

SECTION-A

Q1. Multiple choice questions: **(1*2=2)**

1. Which technology reduces latency by processing data close to where it is generated?

a) IoT
b) 5G
c) Edge Computing
d) Machine Learning

2. What will 6G networks succeed in the evolution of mobile networks?

a) 4G
b) 5G
c) IoT
d) 1G

Q2. Fill in the blanks: **(1*2=2)**

1. ______ enables continuous connectivity for smart homes and connected vehicles.
2. ______ is the next generation of mobile networks expected to follow 5G.

Q3. True or False: **(1*2=2)**

1. AI in mobile computing powers network optimization and personalized services.
2. 1G networks introduced high-speed mobile internet.

SECTION-B

Q4. Very Short answers type questions-I **(2*3=6)**

1. Define IoT and give one example of its application in mobile computing.
2. What is the role of Edge Computing in mobile networks?
3. Mention one future trend that will shape the development of mobile networks.

SECTION-C

Q5. Short answers type questions-II **(4*2=8)**

1. Compare the evolution of mobile networks from 1G to 5G, focusing on improvements in communication.
2. How does AI contribute to improving the mobile computing experience?

SECTION-D

Q6. Long answers type questions **(5*1=5)**

1. Discuss the significance of IoT and Edge Computing in modern mobile networks and explain how these technologies support time-sensitive applications.

Chapter 11 - Viva Voce

Question 1: What is the significance of corporate social responsibility (CSR) in the workplace?
Answer: CSR ensures that companies act ethically, balancing profitability with social and environmental responsibilities.

Question 2: What is the role of cultural sensitivity in international business ethics?
Answer: It ensures respect for local customs and norms, helping avoid conflicts and ethical issues in a globalised world.

Question 3: Define intellectual property in a professional context.
Answer: Intellectual property refers to creations of the mind, like inventions, designs, and artistic works, protected by law.

Question 4: What is whistle-blowing in an organisational context?
Answer: Whistle-blowing is reporting unethical or illegal activities within an organisation to authorities.

Question 5: Why is active listening important in communication?
Answer: Active listening improves understanding and helps build stronger professional relationships.

Question 6: How can AI lead to ethical challenges?
Answer: AI can perpetuate bias in decision-making and may lead to privacy concerns or job displacement.

Question 7: What is the difference between leadership and management?
Answer: Leadership involves inspiring and guiding, while management plans and organises resources.

Question 8: What are the ethical implications of data privacy in technology?
Answer: It involves protecting users' data from unauthorised access, ensuring transparency, and preventing misuse.

Question 9: What is emotional intelligence, and why is it important?
Answer: Emotional intelligence is the ability to recognise and manage emotions, essential for building professional relationships.

Question 10: What is the importance of cross-cultural communication?
Answer: It helps professionals effectively interact and collaborate with people from diverse cultural backgrounds.

Question 11: How does ethical decision-making differ from regular decision-making?
Answer: Ethical decision-making considers the impact on stakeholders, fairness, and adherence to moral principles.

Question 12: Why is adaptability a crucial professional skill?
Answer: Adaptability allows professionals to stay relevant and thrive in a rapidly changing environment.

Question 13: What are the main elements of professional conduct and etiquette?
Answer: Respect, politeness, punctuality, and adherence to workplace norms.

Question 14: How do critical thinking skills help in ethical decision-making?
Answer: Critical thinking helps in analysing situations, identifying biases, and making informed, ethical choices.

Question 15: What are the principles of professional ethics?
Answer: Confidentiality, integrity, fairness, and responsibility are core principles of professional ethics.

Question 16: What is project management, and why is it important?
Answer: Project management involves efficiently planning, executing, and monitoring projects to achieve specific goals.

Question 17: How does ethical leadership impact an organisation?
Answer: Ethical leadership promotes a culture of trust, accountability, and fairness, leading to long-term success.

Question 18: Why is public speaking an essential skill in the workplace?
Answer: It enhances the ability to present ideas clearly and influence others in meetings, presentations, and conferences.

Question 19: What are the challenges of ethics in artificial intelligence?
Answer: Bias in AI algorithms, lack of transparency, and data privacy concerns are significant challenges.

Question 20: How does time management contribute to professional success?
Answer: Effective time management allows professionals to prioritise tasks, meet deadlines, and enhance productivity.

Question 21: What is ethical relativism?
Answer: Ethical relativism suggests that moral principles vary across cultures and should be understood within cultural contexts.

Question 22: What are the components of a professional portfolio?
Answer: A professional portfolio includes achievements, certifications, projects, and skills showcasing qualifications.

Question 23: How does conflict resolution benefit teamwork?
Answer: It helps to resolve disputes, improve collaboration, and maintain a harmonious work environment.

Question 24: What is the significance of ethics in digital and remote work environments?
Answer: It ensures that employees maintain professionalism, confidentiality, and respect for digital tools and data.

Question 25: What is the purpose of codes of ethics in professions?
Answer: Codes of ethics provide guidelines for maintaining integrity and ethical behaviour in professional practice.

Question 26: What role does sustainability play in technology ethics?
Answer: Sustainability focuses on minimising environmental impact while driving technological innovation.

Question 27: Why is goal setting necessary in career planning?
Answer: Goal setting provides direction, motivation, and a clear professional growth and success pathway.

Question 28: How does diversity and inclusion benefit workplaces?
Answer: Valuing different perspectives promotes creativity, innovation, and a more harmonious work environment.

Question 29: What are the ethical concerns related to social media?
Answer: Privacy issues, misinformation, and spreading harmful content are vital ethical concerns in social media use.

Question 30: How do legal responsibilities affect professionals?
Answer: Legal responsibilities ensure that professionals comply with laws, avoid liabilities, and maintain ethical conduct.

Question 31: How does empathy contribute to emotional intelligence?
Answer: Empathy allows professionals to understand and relate to others' emotions, fostering better relationships.

Question 32: What are some common logical fallacies in ethical analysis?
Answer: Ad hominem, false dilemma, and appeal to authority are common logical fallacies that distort ethical reasoning.

Question 33: What is the importance of confidentiality in professional ethics?
Answer: Confidentiality protects sensitive information, builds trust, and ensures ethical responsibility in professional interactions.

Question 34: What is delegation, and how does it empower teams?
Answer: Delegation involves assigning tasks to others, empowering them to take responsibility and develop new skills.

Question 35: Why is reflective practice important in lifelong learning?
Answer: Reflective practice helps professionals assess their progress, learn from experiences, and continuously improve.

Question 36: How does whistle-blowing protect ethical standards in an organisation?
Answer: It exposes unethical or illegal activities, ensuring accountability and promoting transparency.

Question 37: What is the role of ethical frameworks in decision-making?
Answer: Ethical frameworks provide a structured approach to making fair, responsible, and morally sound decisions.

Question 38: Why are case studies critical in understanding ethical dilemmas?
Answer: Case studies provide real-world examples illustrating ethical decisions' complexities and consequences.

Question 39: What is the role of feedback in professional development?
Answer: Feedback helps professionals improve their performance, refine their skills, and achieve better results.

Question 40: How do companies address harassment and discrimination in the workplace?
Answer: Companies establish policies, provide training, and implement reporting mechanisms to prevent and address these issues.

Question 41: What is the significance of analysing ethical scenarios?
Answer: It helps professionals practice making ethical decisions and understand the impact of their choices in real-life situations.

Question 42: How does cyber security impact ethical technology use?
Answer: Cyber security ensures personal data protection, prevents breaches, and promotes responsible use of technology.

Question 43: How do networking skills contribute to professional growth?
Answer: Networking helps professionals build relationships, exchange ideas, and create opportunities for career advancement.

Question 44: What is the impact of global standards on ethical practices?
Answer: Global standards ensure consistency and fairness in ethical practices across industries and regions.

Question 45: Why is leadership integrity important in ethical practices?
Answer: Integrity in leadership builds trust, sets a positive example, and ensures that ethical practices are followed throughout the organisation.

Question 46: What is the purpose of ethical reporting mechanisms?
Answer: Ethical reporting mechanisms allow employees to report misconduct or unethical behaviour without fear of retaliation.

Question 47: How can professionals mitigate bias in decision-making?
Answer: Recognizing potential biases, using diverse perspectives, and applying ethical frameworks to decisions.

Question 48: How does critical thinking help in identifying biases?
Answer: Critical thinking allows individuals to evaluate information objectively and recognise personal or societal biases.

Question 49: What are the ethical implications of environmental sustainability in technology?
Answer: It requires balancing innovation with minimising environmental harm and ensuring responsible resource use.

Question 50: What is the importance of compliance with industry standards?
Answer: Compliance ensures that professionals meet legal requirements and ethical guidelines, maintaining accountability.

Chapter 12 - Project and Case Study

Project Title: Ethical Leadership in a Multinational Corporation

Objective: Analyze the role of ethical leadership in promoting ethical practices across global teams and ensuring integrity and accountability at every level.

1. Project Components1. Leadership Ethics Overview
  a. Description: Assess the ethical framework applied by leadership in multinational corporations.
  b. Key Areas: Ethical decision-making, integrity, accountability.

2. Promoting Ethical Practices
  a. Description: Explore how leaders establish and enforce ethical guidelines across diverse teams.
  b. Actions: Develop a code of conduct, ethical training programs, and ethical reporting mechanisms.

3. Balancing Profitability and Ethics
  a. Description: Evaluate how leaders balance ethical practices while maintaining profitability.
  b. Actions: Create frameworks to assess ethical impacts on profit and long-term sustainability.

4. Integrity and Accountability
  a. Description: Ensure that leadership adheres to ethical standards and remains accountable for their actions.
  b. Actions: Implement leadership assessment protocols for transparency and integrity.

2. Case Study: Ethical Leadership in a Global Organization

Scenario: A multinational company faces challenges with ethical practices across different regions. Leadership promotes a culture of ethics while balancing profitability and managing diverse global teams.

Tasks:

1. Leadership Ethics Assessment

a. Objective: Review the ethical standards currently upheld by leadership.
b. Outcome: Identify gaps and areas for improvement in ethical leadership.

2. Establishing Ethical Guidelines

a. Objective: Develop an ethical framework that is applicable across all regions.
b. Outcome: Implement a unified code of ethics and training programs.

3. Profit and Ethics Balance

a. Objective: Balance ethical practices with profitability.
b. Outcome: Sustainable business strategies maintaining ethical integrity.

Chapter 13 - Sample Exam Paper

General Instructions:
Time Allowed: 3 Hours
Maximum Marks: 100
Answer all the questions.
Marks are indicated against each question.

SECTION-A

I. Multiple Choice Questions **(2*5=10 Marks)**

1. Which of the following best defines professional ethics?

a) Personal beliefs about right and wrong
b) societal norms and customs
c) Standards governing professional conduct
d) Legal requirements set by the government

2. Active listening is characterised by:

a) Interrupting the speaker to offer solutions
b) Paying full attention and providing feedback
c) Preparing your response while the speaker is talking
d) Agreeing with everything the speaker says

3. Emotional intelligence refers to:

a) Suppressing your emotions
b) Understanding and managing your own and others' emotions
c) Using emotions to manipulate others
d) avoiding emotional situations

4. Corporate Social Responsibility (CSR) focuses on:

a) Maximizing shareholder profits
b) A company's efforts to contribute to societal goals
c) Compliance with legal standards only
d) Internal policies on employee behaviour

5. Which technology reduces latency by processing data near its source?

a) Cloud Computing
b) Edge Computing
c) Machine Learning
d) IoT

II. Fill in the Blanks **(2*5=10 Marks)**

1. The process of managing time efficiently to meet deadlines is known as __________.
2. The concept of balancing profitability and ethics is often referred to as __________.
3. In the context of cross-cultural communication, __________ refers to the ability to understand and respect cultural differences.
4. A decision-making framework that focuses on ethical dilemmas using rules and principles is called __________.
5. The practice of critically reflecting on your own actions and decisions in a professional setting is known as __________.

SECTION-B

III. Very Short Answer Type Questions-I **(4*5=20 Marks)**

1. Define professional ethics and explain its importance in the workplace.
2. How does active listening contribute to effective communication?
3. Explain the term empathy in the context of professional relationships.

4. What is whistle blowing and its significance in maintaining workplace ethics?
5. Describe the role of time management in leadership and decision-making.

SECTION-C

IV. Short Answer Type Questions-II **(6*5= 30 Marks)**

1. Discuss the main differences between verbal and non-verbal communication.
2. How does emotional intelligence impact leadership and teamwork?
3. What is ethical decision-making? Describe any two ethical frameworks used in decision-making.
4. Analyze how corporate social responsibility (CSR) can benefit society and an organization.
5. How do ethical challenges arise in the use of emerging technologies like AI and cyber security?

SECTION-D:

V. Long Answer Type Questions **(10*3=30 Marks)**

1. Evaluate how effective communication and interpersonal skills can help resolve conflicts in a diverse team. Include examples of barriers and strategies for overcoming them. (10 marks)
2. Discuss the role of ethical leadership in addressing challenges related to data privacy and cyber security in modern organization. Use relevant examples to support your answer. (10 marks)
3. What are the long-term benefits for organizations that implement ethical leadership practices in managing cyber security and data privacy risks? (10 marks)

Video Resources

IGNOU Cloud Computing and IoT Previous Years Solved Papers Playlist.
Link: https://www.youtube.com/playlist?list=PLzlh_31VWEFoJ3LBMfwQAqJ_sL7aJH0-F

Scan for Qr code:

Cloud Computing Playlist.
Link: https://www.youtube.com/playlist?list=PLzlh_31VWEFpK71LTz5Sa8mEhbkvrdyqk

Scan for QR Code:

Cloud Computing Interview Playlist.
Link: https://www.youtube.com/playlist?list=PLzlh_31VWEFptljMGPrdoFTkWvwL7e7lz

Scan for QR Code:

© Author and Publisher 2024